IMAGES
of America

ROUTE 66 IN TULSA

The majestic Meadow Gold sign advertising the dairy products of Beatrice Foods has been a cornerstone of Tulsa's historic Route 66 since 1934. This view shows the impressive neon at its original location on the southwest corner of Eleventh Street and Lewis Avenue. In the early 2000s, the sign was dismantled, restored, and relocated two miles west. Today's travelers will recognize this corner as the location of Mother Road Market. (Courtesy of Beryl Ford Collection/Rotary Club of Tulsa.)

On the Cover: Tulsa's Blue Dome service station, on the southwest corner of Second Street and Elgin Avenue, was on the first alignment of Route 66. The design by Lawrence Blue and Fred Knoblock for Chastain Oil Company resembles the Hagia Sophia Grand Mosque in Istanbul, Turkey. Opening in 1925, the station pioneered customer conveniences, including pressurized air, restrooms, and 24-hour service. Operating as a Gulf station from the time of this 1949 photograph into the 1960s, this symbol of Tulsa's oil affluence now anchors the vibrant Blue Dome Historic District. (Courtesy of Beryl Ford Collection/Rotary Club of Tulsa.)

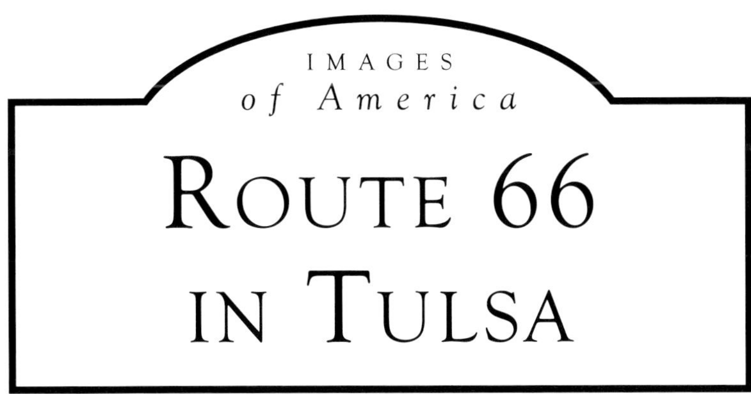

Steve Clem and Becky Hatchett
Foreword by Rhys Martin

ISBN 9781467162197
Hardcover ISBN 9781540299642

Published by Arcadia Publishing
Charleston, South Carolina

Printed in the United States of America

Library of Congress Control Number: 2025930360

For all general information, please contact Arcadia Publishing:
Telephone 843-853-2070
Fax 843-853-0044
E-mail sales@arcadiapublishing.com

Visit us on the Internet at www.arcadiapublishing.com

I dedicate this book to all the individuals, past and present, who have worked on Tulsa's Historic Route 66, serving travelers and dispensing hometown hospitality to all who pause here.

—Steve Clem

I wish to dedicate this book to the volunteers and visitors from all over the world at the Route 66 Historical Village.

—Becky Hatchett

Contents

Foreword

Route 66 is a romantic idea for many people—a tie to the past, when life was simpler and people took joy in the experience of travel. But that, itself, is a simplified version of the truth. When the US 66 Highway was established in 1926, it was in the service of making travel easier, which it did. But the interstate highway system made it even easier at the expense of the communities that the original road had helped develop.

If you stick to Interstate 44 in Tulsa, you will cruise through in just a few minutes but miss out on so much of what makes the city a special place. For many years, Route 66 in Tulsa was just another street, a ghost of a bygone era. But starting in the mid-2000s, with direct investment by the City of Tulsa, Tulsa's close history with arguably the most famous highway in the world was elevated.

What started with sidewalk pavers and zoning overlays and a few bronze plaques has become a whirlwind of activity and attractions that have earned the city the title "Capital of Route 66." A Neon Sign Grant Program has brought about the illumination of the corridor. The giant legacy of the road has brought other giants to the roadside, like Buck Atom and Meadow Gold Mack. Longtime local businesses have relocated to the Main Street of America to be a part of something special. People from all over the world stop in Tulsa and marvel at the richness of our story.

For me, it was the removal of the iconic Meadow Gold neon sign from its home at Eleventh Street and Lewis Avenue that turned me on to Route 66. I thought we had lost something important, and I had not been paying enough attention. Of course, I was relieved when I discovered it was being restored and rebuilt two miles to the west. But it inspired me to look deeper and take a little road trip. What I found was more than a footnote in American history: it was a linear community, very much alive. And its history is still being written.

—Rhys Martin
President, Oklahoma Route 66 Association
Commissioner, Tulsa Route 66 Commission

Acknowledgments

The authors extend their gratitude to the following individuals who made this book possible: To Michael Wallis, Suzanne Fitzgerald Wallis, Rhys Martin, Ken Busby, and Jim Hinckley for their extreme generosity in sharing their time and wealth of knowledge. To Luke Williams and the Tulsa Historical Society and Museum, now known as the Museum of Tulsa History, whose various collections contributed a large percentage of the photographs in this book; many are courtesy of the Beryl Ford Collection/Rotary Club of Tulsa/Tulsa City-County Library/Tulsa Historical Society and Museum. We also thank the Tulsa City-County Central Library for the use of its wonderful resources in the Oklahoma Room; Jim Ross and Shellee Graham for information and photographs and for being the gold standard in all they do; postcard collectors Joe Sonderman, Mike Ward, and Steve Rider for sharing items from their extensive collections to this project; and Joy Ryker for Westside service station photographs from her family's collection.

The authors would like to thank the following additional individuals representing the libraries, archives, and historical societies that have preserved Route 66 photographs and made them accessible to us for this book: Jon D. May, photograph archivist, Oklahoma Historical Society (including the Oklahoma Department of Transportation Collection); Melissa Kunz, director of Special Collections, the University of Tulsa McFarlin Library; Jessica Castaño, Department of Special Collections and University Archives, the University of Tulsa McFarlin Library (including the Robert McCormack Photostudio Archive); Sheena Perez, Cyrus Stevens Avery Archive, Oklahoma State University-Tulsa Library; Nicholas B. Fry, John W. Barriger III National Railway Library, University of Missouri–St. Louis; Robert W. McKnight, head of Transportation Collections at the St. Louis Mercantile Library; Steve Robinson, board chair, Claremore Museum of History; Roy and Sherry Heim, Southwest Tulsa Historical Society; and the Newberry Library and the Library of Congress.

Steve would like to thank Susan Yates, Mary Beth Babcock, Terri and Archie Fain, William Franklin, Sheila Mears-Smith, Melissa Winterscheid, Jeannie Bagwell, Leslie McDaniel, Kathy Anderson, and Brady A. Wilson.

Becky would like to thank Donna Savage and David Breed.

Thank you to Maggie Brown; we miss your daily participation in preserving Tulsa's history.

Introduction

A person could travel Route 66's 2,448 miles through eight states, from Chicago to the Santa Monica Pier, learn the fascinating histories of cities large and small, and not encounter a story anything like the one Tulsa, Oklahoma, has to tell.

For starters, US Highway 66 was conceived in Tulsa by the man who is now called "the Father of Route 66," Cyrus "Cy" Avery. He came to the oil boom town the same year that Oklahoma became the 46th state in 1907.

Tulsa's first settlers were Indigenous tribes who were forced from their ancestral lands in the southeastern states to Indian Territory in each tribe's version of the Trail of Tears. The "lower" Muscogee Creeks settled along the Arkansas River at present Tulsa in 1836. A trading post and cattle ranch were later established in the area. The arrival of the railroads in the 1880s brought more settlers, and the first businesses were established. Tulsa was incorporated in 1898.

The cow town of Tulsa became transformed through oil discoveries, in Red Fork in 1901, then in the prolific Glenn Pool in 1905. An influx of people arrived to make their fortunes in oil. The boom was on! Tulsa's population soared from 1,390 citizens in 1900 to 18,182 by 1910 and to a whopping 72,075 persons in 1920. Tulsa was the headquarters for oil companies and oilmen whose work and philanthropy created a "Magic City," with an emphasis on culture and the arts.

It was in this environment that Cy Avery established himself as an astute businessman and effective civic leader. Avery worked in the Better Roads movement of the 1910s and early 1920s, born of the lack of adequate highways for a nation newly mobile. In the mid-1920s, Avery played a pivotal role in the creation of the numbered national highway system. Through that process, he championed an east-to-west route from Chicago to Los Angeles that, not coincidentally, passed through his adopted hometown.

The story of how that route ended up with the number "66" has twists and turns worthy of the road itself, as it winds through the eight states of Illinois, Missouri, Kansas, Oklahoma, Texas, New Mexico, Arizona, and California.

Route 66 officially came into being on November 11, 1926. But Cyrus Avery's influence on the road did not end there. The following year, he formed the US 66 Highway Association to promote the route to the public and facilitate the paving of the entire 2,448 miles, which took another decade to complete.

It is helpful to understand Route 66's different alignments in different eras. Simply stated, the earliest route followed section lines as it zigzagged through the eight states, with many 90-degree turns as it respected property lines. Subsequent alignments made the route straighter and wider.

In Tulsa, the earliest alignment, 1926–1932, passed Cyrus Avery's gas station and restaurant complex east of town, came down Admiral Place, and then jogged to Second Street past the Moorish-style Blue Dome service station, passing through the heart of downtown before zigzagging to the Eleventh Street bridge.

Those first Route 66 travelers would have found a city just becoming the "Oil Capital of the World." A Roaring Twenties building boom created the skyline and architecture that would define Tulsa for decades. If Route 66 motorists glanced northward at Greenwood Avenue, they would have witnessed the rebuilding of the Greenwood community, two blocks away, after what is known as the 1921 Tulsa Race Massacre—a shameful chapter that the city and its people still grapple with over a century later.

The 1932–1959 alignment (Eleventh Street) is considered Route 66's heyday. The highway entered from the east on 193rd Street, turned west on Eleventh Street, and remained there to the Eleventh Street bridge. This classic alignment skirted the edge of downtown through what is now called the Cathedral district. Once across the Eleventh Street bridge, the route, unchanged from 1926 to 1959, passed refineries and railroad yards, Westside neighborhoods, and Crystal City Amusement Park.

Throughout the route's 59-year existence as America's way west, there was something special about those double sixes—maybe it was the beauty of the vistas as US 66 sliced through the Ozarks of Missouri or the way the sky seemed to open when a traveler entered New Mexico and Arizona, whose sunsets lingered in the mind's eye long after the last ray of light disappeared beneath the horizon. Most assuredly, it had something to do with the people making a living on the route in the heart of America, making travelers feel welcome many miles from home.

Out of all the numbered roads in the highway system, US Route 66 was the one that captured the public's imagination repeatedly, through literature, film, music, and television. In the 1939 novel *The Grapes of Wrath*, John Steinbeck called Route 66 "the Mother Road," the road of flight for those devastated by the Great Depression and the Dust Bowl. It was the route used for troops and supplies during World War II. It was the path that inspired songwriter Bobby Troup to compose a catchy ditty urging listeners to "Get Your Kicks on Route 66." It was the road that launched a thousand family vacations and the one chosen by Buzz and Todd in their Corvette as they acted out their morality plays on the hit television series *Route 66*.

In 1959, with the completion of Interstate 44 on the southern outskirts of Tulsa, Route 66 moved over to Interstate 44, called 66 Bypass and Skelly Bypass, for its path bypassing the city. With Route 66 traffic gone from the city routes and Tulsa's population shifting to the suburbs, the mom-and-pop businesses and the neighborhoods along those routes began their decades-long decline. In Tulsa, the Mother Road's move to Interstate 44 coincided with the coming of corporate chain motels and restaurants that supplanted unique, family-owned businesses.

Once Route 66 was bypassed by the interstate system in all eight states, the Chicago to Los Angeles route was discontinued—decertified in 1985.

When US Highway 66 no longer appeared on any map, there was a void—a feeling that something important had disappeared from the nation's identity. Route 66's passing into history marked the end of holding America close and hearing her heartbeat.

Prolific journalist Michael Wallis, born and raised near an alignment of Route 66 in St. Louis, relocated to Tulsa with his wife, Suzanne Fitzgerald Wallis, in the early 1980s and began researching and writing the books that would establish Wallis as a premier authority on the American West.

His 1990 release *Route 66: The Mother Road* struck a chord with those feeling the loss of the Main Street of America. Wallis's love letter informed readers that most of the route was still out there and drivable, as were the people who made it special.

Wallis's book sold one million copies and earned him the first of his three Pulitzer Prize nominations. But the book accomplished something even more remarkable—it spawned the renaissance of Route 66!

Early voices in the pursuit to revive old Highway 66 included Angel Delgadillo, who formed the first state association in Seligman, Arizona, in 1987, seeking historic signage for the route. Quinta Scott and Susan Croce Kelly teamed up for a photographic essay, *Route 66: The Highway and its People*, in 1988. Wallis's success coalesced these efforts, and those of others, into a unified movement to resurrect the Mother Road.

One of the fans of Wallis's book was filmmaker John Lasseter of Pixar Animation Studios, then chief creative officer for Pixar, the animation studio behind *Toy Story*. Lasseter contacted

Wallis about an idea for a movie centered around Route 66. Wallis signed on as a consultant, leading Pixar's creative teams down Route 66 to get inspiration from locales and characters for what became the first *Cars* movie. Lasseter and the development team so loved Wallis's voice that they cast him as the character of the Sheriff of Radiator Springs, which Wallis has played in three *Cars* films to date.

Wallis describes Route 66 as a linear community. In this context, Tulsa's historic role was as an important stopover—roughly a day's drive from St. Louis to the east and to Amarillo to the west. The Oil Capital offered visitors a variety of tourist services along with larger city amenities like department store shopping and grand movie palaces. For many, Tulsa was a place to pause—for fuel, a meal, a few hours' sleep, and perhaps to have some fun.

For the past 35 years, Wallis has been the face of Tulsa's Route 66 rebirth at event after event, from the rededication of the Sue A. Bland No. 1 historical marker near the spot of Tulsa's first oil strike to the dedication of the Cyrus Avery Route 66 Memorial Bridge and the launch parties for the new attractions Buck Atom Space Cowboy and Stella Atom.

On December 28, 2022, US president Joe Biden appointed Wallis to the Route 66 Centennial Commission, giving the man responsible for Route 66's renaissance a prestigious role in planning the road's 100-year celebration.

In these pages, a reference to Historic Route 66 means the two different city routes through Tulsa before the Mother Road moved to Interstate 44 in 1959. The Historic Route 66 signs throughout the heart of the city reflect this. There are 28 miles total on the two historical alignments, which are bookended by gateways on the east and west ends.

Oklahoma has more drivable miles of Route 66 than any other state—over 400 total. Part of the reason Route 66 has been preserved in this part of the state is because it has been the "free road" alternative to the toll roads—the Will Rogers Turnpike, from the Missouri state line to Tulsa, and the Turner Turnpike, from Tulsa to Oklahoma City. Today, the "free road" is signed as State Highway 66 (SH-66), as is the segment of Interstate 44 between the two turnpikes.

In this book, the following names are used interchangeably: Route 66, US 66, Highway 66, the Mother Road, and "the Main Street of America" as well as the name that honors Oklahoma's favorite son, "the Will Rogers Highway." Route 66 assumed that name months after the actor, humorist, and newspaper columnist's tragic death in a plane crash in August 1935. Tulsa is Will Rogers country—30 miles from the humorist's birthplace of Oologah and 30 minutes from the Will Rogers Memorial in Claremore east on Route 66.

Many of the historic photographs in this book are from the Beryl Ford Collection. Everyone who enjoys learning about Tulsa's days gone by owes a debt of gratitude to Ford, who died in 2009 at age 83. An amateur historian, Ford loved to photograph Tulsa intersections. This could be dangerous work, especially on Route 66, which carried the traffic of the nation. It is said that Ford liked to photograph on Sundays when traffic was light. It was not only safer, but there were fewer obstacles (vehicles) to capturing the businesses on each corner.

In 2024, Tulsa was officially named the Capital of Route 66. Due to public and private investment and entrepreneurs such as Mary Beth Babcock, the brains behind Buck Atom, Stella, and a lot more, Tulsa's historic routes again flourish. There is an eclectic blend of old and new: from repurposed gas stations to classic lodging; Art Deco architecture to muffler man giants; and fun attractions, including Mother Road Market, Cyrus Avery Centennial Plaza, and Route 66 Historical Village.

Thanks to the Tulsa Route 66 Commission's Neon Sign Grant Program, brilliant neon once again illuminates the night on the historic routes.

The pages that follow document the history of Route 66 in Tulsa and demonstrate how the former Oil Capital has emerged as the Capital of Route 66.

One

A Bridge to the Future

Cyrus Avery, the Father of Route 66

In the 1910s, as Henry Ford's Model T was making the automobile affordable to the average American, owners were anxious to hit the road. However, highways were dismal. Cities were linked by a system of trails, most unpaved, with no standards in roadbuilding, maintenance, or naming. Signage was inconsistent. If navigating these rutted trails in an automobile was not difficult enough, whenever it rained, the road turned to mud, and traffic stopped.

The public's outcry for better roads created a Good Roads Movement, for which Cyrus Stevens Avery, a Tulsa businessman and civic leader, became a leading voice. Avery was a visionary who recognized the need for a system of paved highways, had a definite plan in mind, and possessed the skills to make it happen.

A persuasive orator, Avery gave speeches and joined trail associations that supported the improvement of existing roads. He sought a government role in roadbuilding, understanding the financial burden it represented to communities.

Avery moved his young family from Vinita, Oklahoma, to the boom town of Tulsa in 1907, the year Oklahoma became a state. He worked in the oil and gas business, real estate, and experimental farming on acreage he acquired a few miles east of town.

A dynamic businessman, Avery's successes helped him get elected county commissioner in 1913. In that role, he brought about a new bridge over the Arkansas River, completed in 1916, linking the business community with the Westside oil fields. A decade after its completion, that concrete-and-steel span helped get US Highway 66 routed through Tulsa. US Highways 64 and 75 also came through the Oil Capital.

Other Avery accomplishments included bringing a reliable water source to Tulsa and helping establish the Tulsa Municipal Airport.

While serving as Oklahoma highway commissioner from 1922 to 1926, Avery was appointed to the Joint Board of Interstate Highways, tasked with designating and numbering US highways. Through regional meetings and written correspondence, highway representatives from around the country devised the first national highway system. To this often-chaotic process, Avery provided leadership, civility, and formidable negotiating skills.

US Highway 66 was officially certified on November 11, 1926. For his role in creating and promoting what he named "the Main Street of America," Cy Avery is honored as the "Father of Route 66."

Cyrus Stevens Avery, known as "Cy," began life in Stevensville, Pennsylvania, in 1871. To escape a depressed economy, Avery's father, A.J., relocated the family to Indian Territory in 1884, when the boy was 13. A.J. and his son worked a farm on Spavinaw Creek, where Cy developed his love for agriculture and the land that would become Oklahoma. Around 1890, A.J. bought land on the Elk River in Missouri. Although Cy's schooling was sporadic, he enrolled at William Jewel College in Liberty, Missouri, near Kansas City. Upon graduation, he married Essie McClelland, a fellow Missourian. Producing three children, the couple would have a long life together, most of it in Tulsa, where they moved in 1907. At left, Avery is shown with his signature. Below, he is pictured with Essie and daughter Helen Louise. (Both, courtesy of Cyrus Stevens Avery Collection/Department of Special Collections and Archives/Oklahoma State University-Tulsa.)

Living in Tulsa, Cyrus Avery became a leading voice in the Good Roads Movement of the 1910s and 1920s. To support the cause, Avery published a monthly magazine, the *Nation's Highways*. The issue shown at right featured the Albert Pike Highway Association. Below is shown the first crossing at Eleventh Street, a wooden toll bridge that Avery played a key role in replacing. (Both, courtesy of Cyrus Stevens Avery Collection/Department of Special Collections and Archives/Oklahoma State University-Tulsa.)

THE NATION'S HIGHWAYS

Volume 1 — Tulsa, Oklahoma, April, 1921 — 10c PER COPY $1.00 PER YEAR — Number

Organizers of The Albert Pike Highway Association in Their Initial Meeting at Tulsa, Okla., January 29th, 1917.

THE 1921 CONVENTION WILL BE HELD AT TULSA, OKLAHOMA IN CONVENTION HALL, APRIL 21, 22 AND 23, AT WHICH TIME IT WILL MEET JOINTLY WITH THE WHITE RIVER TRAIL ASSOCIATION AND THE ASSOCIATED HIGHWAYS OF AMERICA.

Avery served as Tulsa County commissioner from 1913 to 1916. A major accomplishment was building a more substantial bridge at Eleventh Street, linking rapidly growing Tulsa to the oil fields and industries on the Westside. Funded by a $200,000 bond issue, at a length of 1,470 feet, it was the longest reinforced-concrete bridge in the Southwest when it opened in 1916. A decade after its completion, the bridge played a crucial role in Avery getting US Highway 66 routed through Tulsa.

When other highway officials preferred a more northern route through the Colorado Rockies for Avery's proposed Chicago to Los Angeles highway, he successfully argued that the route would have to cross the Arkansas River somewhere, and Tulsa already had the best concrete bridge to accommodate the traffic, thus saving the cost of constructing a new one. (Courtesy of Mike Ward.)

In the early 1920s, as a member of the Tulsa Water Board, Avery helped solve Tulsa's drinking water problem through the creation of the Spavinaw Water Project. It involved damming water from the area Avery had enjoyed as a child in Spavinaw, Oklahoma, and transporting it through a 55-mile pipeline to Tulsa. When completed, it was the longest gravity-flow water pipeline in the United States. (Courtesy of Mike Ward.)

EXPERIENCE RECORD

Citizen of Tulsa since 1907.

1913-1916—Elected County Commissioner. Chairman two terms.

1918—World War 1 Co. Mgr. Liberty Loan Drives.

1918—On Nov. 1, 1918, appointed U. S. Agriculture Adviser to Dist. Ex. Board Eastern Div. No. 2 and had charge of 23 counties in Eastern Oklahoma.

1921-1924—Member of Board which built Spavinaw Water System. (Salary $1.00 per year).

1924-1927—Chairman of First State Highway Commission which organized present Highway System.

1925—Appointed by Bureau of Public Roads as Member of Board for laying out and creating present U. S. Highway System. Member of Sub-Committee of 5 which allotted to the roads the numbers which they bear today.

1928—Member of Executive Committee that built Tulsa Airport.

1928—Member of Underwriters Committee that purchased Mohawk Park land.

1935—W.P.A. Director, District No. 1, 13 Counties N. E. Oklahoma.

(OVER)

In 1924, Avery became the Oklahoma state highway commissioner, which made him Oklahoma's representative to the American Association of State Highway Officials (AASHO). That gave him a national voice in the movement. Avery was chosen for the board that created the national highway system and the subcommittee that numbered them, accomplishments that he later included on his resume, above. (Courtesy of Cyrus Stevens Avery Collection/Department of Special Collections and Archives/Oklahoma State University-Tulsa.)

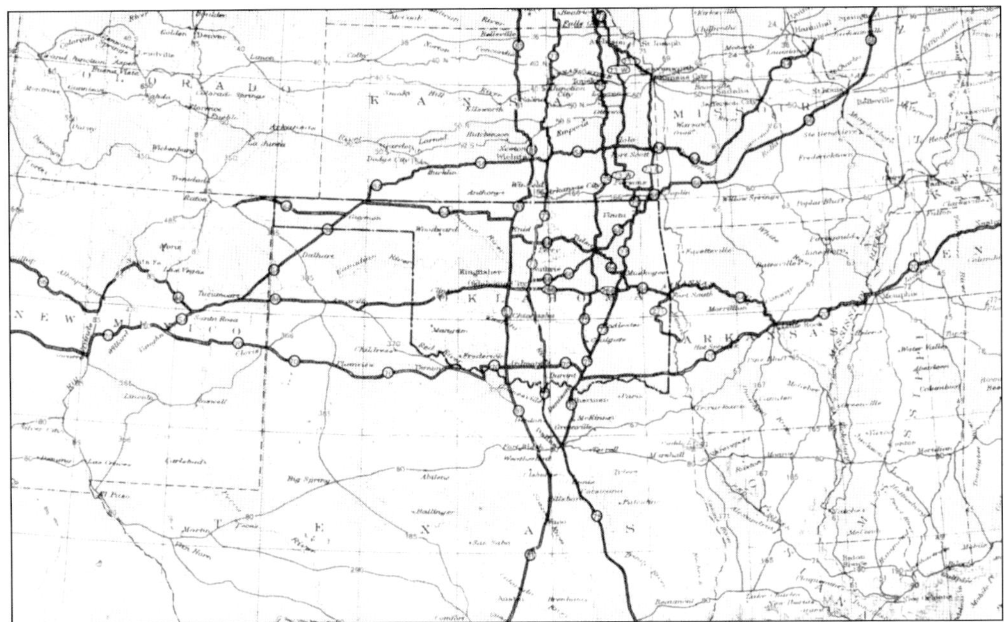

For the new highway system, above, north-south roads received odd numbers and east-west routes were given even numbers. Since two-digit numbers ending in zero were reserved for major east-west arteries, the number 60 was assigned to Avery's Los Angeles to Chicago route. However, the governor of Kentucky protested—arguing that 60 be used for a highway through his state. Washington, DC, highway officials asked Avery to find a solution. Avery gave up the number 60 but refused the replacement number 62. Looking to see what digits were unassigned, Oklahoma chief highway engineer John M. Page discovered the number 66 had not been taken, and Avery loved the idea. On April 30, 1926, Avery and Missouri's B.H. Piepmeier sent this now-famous telegram agreeing to a number change from 60 to 66. (Above, courtesy of Cyrus Stevens Avery Collection/Department of Special Collections and Archives/Oklahoma State University-Tulsa; below, courtesy of Judy Walker.)

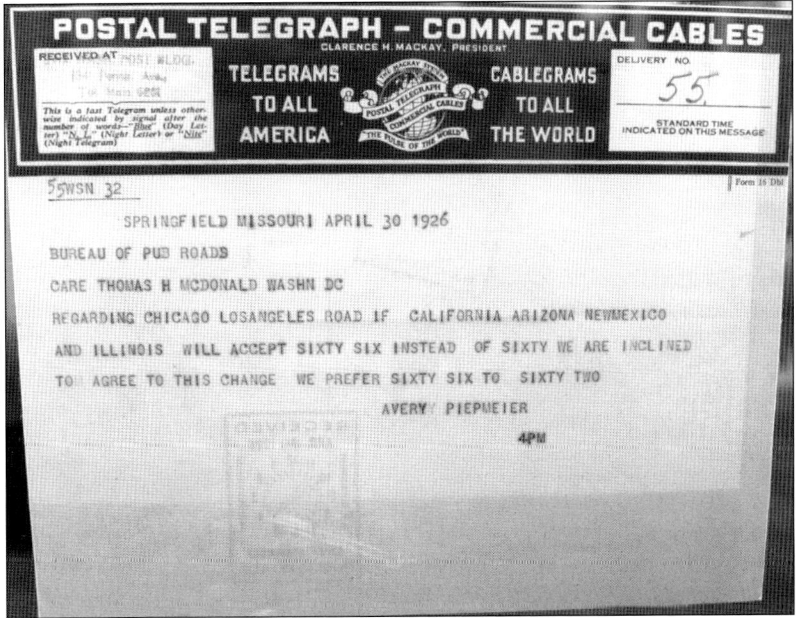

POSTAL TELEGRAPH - COMMERCIAL CABLES

CLARENCE H. MACKAY, PRESIDENT

RECEIVED AT

This is a fast Telegram unless otherwise indicated by signal after the number of words—"Blue" (Day Letter) "N.L." (Night Letter) or "Nite" (Night Telegram)

TELEGRAMS TO ALL AMERICA

THE MACKAY SYSTEM · POSTAL TELEGRAPH · COMMERCIAL CABLES · THE PULSE OF THE WORLD

CABLEGRAMS TO ALL THE WORLD

DELIVERY NO. 55

STANDARD TIME INDICATED ON THIS MESSAGE

55WSN 32

Form 16 Dbl

SPRINGFIELD MISSOURI APRIL 30 1926

BUREAU OF PUB ROADS

CARE THOMAS H MCDONALD WASHN DC

REGARDING CHICAGO LOSANGELES ROAD IF CALIFORNIA ARIZONA NEWMEXICO AND ILLINOIS WILL ACCEPT SIXTY SIX INSTEAD OF SIXTY WE ARE INCLINED TO AGREE TO THIS CHANGE WE PREFER SIXTY SIX TO SIXTY TWO

AVERY PIEPMEIER

4PM

In 1927, Avery established the US 66 Highway Association to market the highway to the public and promote paving the entire route. Here is the association's rarely seen 1934 promotional emblem, which was printed on metal and distributed to motorists in the eight Route 66 states. It was meant to be attached to cars, like a license plate, to promote Highway 66. (Courtesy of Kathy Anderson, Anderson Productions.)

At age 87, Cyrus Avery received word that River Road between Tulsa and Sand Springs would be renamed Avery Drive. Forty years earlier, as Tulsa County commissioner, Avery had cleared a portion of that scenic two-lane road along the Arkansas River. Avery died in 1963 at age 91 and was posthumously honored as the "Father of Route 66." (Courtesy of Cyrus Stevens Avery Collection/Department of Special Collections and Archives/Oklahoma State University-Tulsa.)

Two

Early Years (1926–1932)

Admiral Place to the Blue Dome

The first alignment of US 66 approached Tulsa from the east on Eleventh Street. Turning north at Mingo Road, five miles out in the country, the route passed Cyrus Avery's gas station, restaurant, and tourist cabins before continuing west. From there it followed Federal Drive (later Admiral Place), passing McIntyre Airport at Sheridan Road.

As Highway 66 neared the city center, it jogged over to Second Street, past the stunning, new Blue Dome Service Station, the region's first 24-hour fueling operation, which introduced conveniences like free air, water, and car washes, performed in its bays that reached out from the center dome like tentacles in two directions.

Turning south at Detroit Avenue, travelers would have found a bustling downtown during a building boom that created structures that would define Tulsa's skyline for decades. By 1930, Tulsa had more structures of 10 or more stories than any city of its size in the world. That included the Philtower, 427 South Boston Avenue, built by Waite Phillips in the Gothic Revival style and embellished with Art Deco details. Other Deco masterpieces from the route's early years include the Tulsa Club building, Boston Avenue United Methodist Church, and the Public Market. Tulsa's population soared from 72,075 persons in 1920 to over 140,000 citizens in the 1930 census.

Through downtown, Highway 66 made several turns along its path to Avery's Eleventh Street bridge.

Tulsa's early alignment of US 66 was the site of two exciting events while it carried the traffic of the nation, in 1927 and 1928, respectively.

Although Route 66 moved one mile south to Eleventh Street in 1932, US 75/State Highway 33 continued to use the Admiral Place corridor. Businesses catering to travelers continued to locate there, in addition to the newer alignment of US 66.

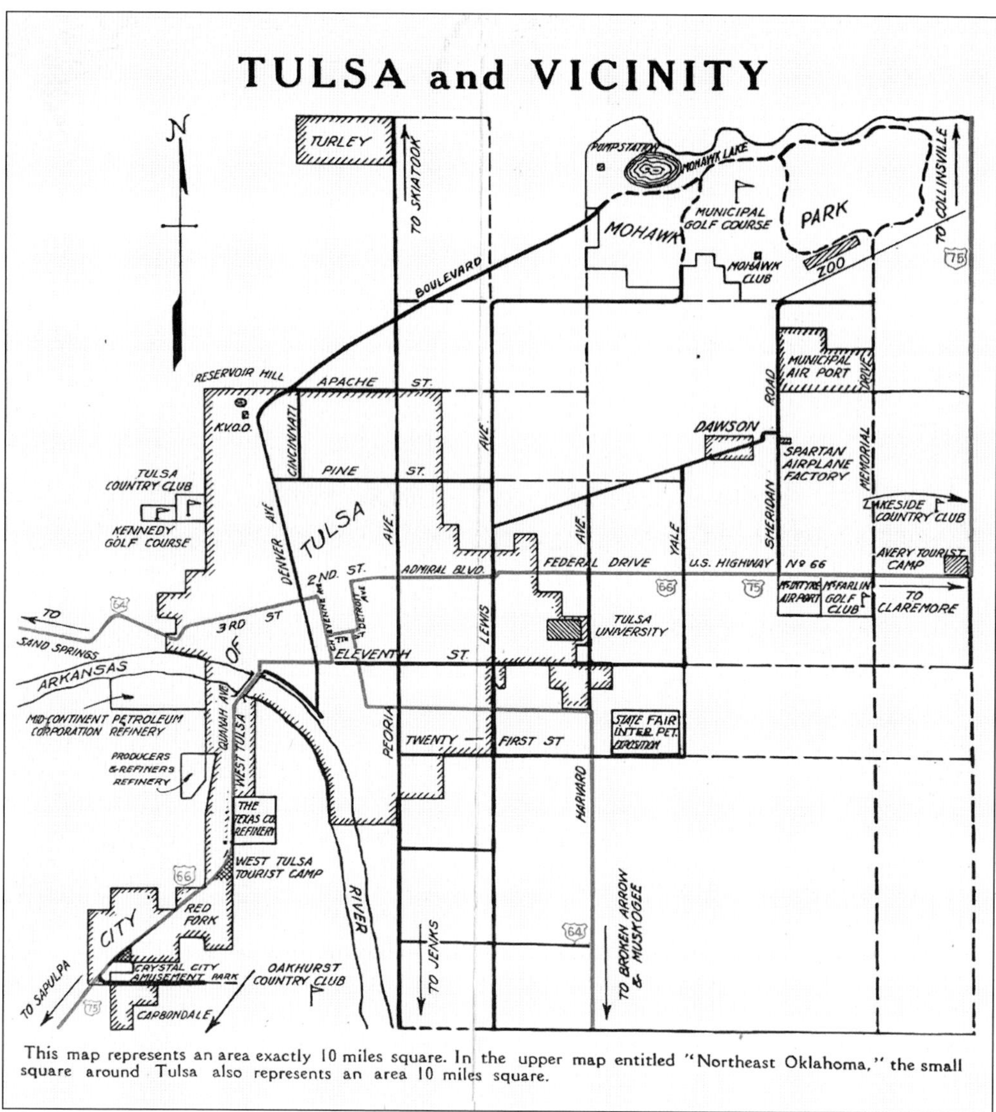

This Tulsa Chamber of Commerce map from November 1928 displays the first alignment (1926–1932) of Route 66 through Tulsa. The rightmost vertical line is Mingo Road, with Cyrus Avery's Tourist Camp shown at Federal Drive/US Highway 66 and Mingo Road. As Highway 66 heads west, Federal Drive becomes Admiral Place, and the route enters downtown on East Second Street. Highway 66 jogs through the business district, turning south at Detroit Avenue, west at Seventh Street, and south at Cheyenne Avenue before heading west to the Eleventh Street bridge. Crossing into the west side, Highway 66 follows Quanah Avenue south past oil refineries, Red Fork, and Crystal City Amusement Park. The map also displays the first paths of US Highways 75 and 64 through the city. The upper right portion of the map shows Tulsa Municipal Airport, which Cyrus Avery had a hand in bringing to fruition in 1928. The following year saw the opening of the Spartan School of Aeronautics, which trained pilots and support personnel. (Courtesy of Route 66 Alliance.)

In the late 1920s, when motorist accommodations consisted of crude cabins and camping, the Pierce Oil Company planned to bring the downtown hotel experience to major US highways. Anticipating the flood of motorists the new federal highway system would bring, the St. Louis–based company began constructing a chain of elaborate tourist "terminals," each with a 40-unit hotel, restaurant, gas station, and a nurse on duty. Designed by Beverly Nelson, who later was the State Department architect in charge of all American buildings in Europe in World War II, Tulsa's Pierce Pennant Terminal opened in 1929, six miles east of the city on Eleventh Street, near 129th East Avenue. However, the Great Depression derailed the company's grand plans, and only a handful were built. Others were in Miami, Oklahoma; Columbia and Rolla, Missouri; and St. Louis. After 1960, when the buildings sat abandoned across from Tulsa East Central High School's stadium, curious students explored the eerie insides of this once swanky tourist hotel. The complex was eventually demolished. (Courtesy of Museum of Tulsa History.)

The early alignment of Highway 66 passed by Cyrus Avery's gas station and restaurant, five miles east of Tulsa, which was positioned in the middle of what is now the intersection of Admiral Place and Mingo Road. It opened in 1924, the year Avery was appointed state highway commissioner. Designed in an English style with a steep tiled roof, the service station faced west, toward town, with the restaurant, Old English Inn, on the opposite side of the two-story building. A 1930s restaurant remodel tripled the eatery's seating capacity. The poultry for the inn's popular chicken dishes came from the surrounding Avery farm. Below, Avery's tourist cabins, located near the complex, provided some of the earliest lodging on Tulsa's Highway 66. (Above, courtesy of Steve Rider; below, courtesy of Museum of Tulsa History.)

"ANDY" PAYNE

EDITION OF THE

OFFICIAL PROGRAM

Andrew Payne crosses the Oklahoma state line ahead

C. C. PYLE'S

First Annual International Trans-Continental Footrace

PRICE 10 CENTS

The US 66 Highway Association sought an event to promote its new highway—something that would capture the public's attention. The association found it in C.C. Pyle's First Annual International Transcontinental Foot Race. Pyle was a promoter in the P.T. Barnum tradition, attracting participants for his Los Angeles to New York slog with a $25,000 cash prize. Most of the route was unpaved. Dubbed as the "bunion derby" by a sportswriter, there were daily accounts of the race's progress in newspapers across the land. Unfortunately, the promoter, Pyle, was more interested in advancing himself than in promoting the highway, and his publicity did not always mention the road. However, the coast-to-coast marathon did capture the public's interest, especially when an Oklahoma Cherokee farm boy, Andy Payne, from Foyil, took the lead, besting famous runners from around the globe. (Courtesy of the Claremore Museum.)

Promoter C.C. Pyle and football star Red Grange traveled by bus, while the runners had motor vehicle support teams. When the entourage reached Tulsa, everyone wanted a glimpse of local favorite Andy Payne, pictured on the right. Payne was declared the winner in New York two months, 22 days after they started. He paid off the family farm and married his girlfriend with his winnings. (Courtesy of the Claremore Museum.)

Moses Village Motel was located at 9700 East Admiral Place. That would have been at Mingo Road in the vicinity of Cyrus Avery's tourist cabins, service station, and restaurant. Nestled in the country in a grove of trees east of town, its advertising invited tourists to "enjoy the serenity of this lovely spot." (Courtesy of Mike Ward.)

One of the biggest events of 1927 in Tulsa occurred right on Route 66. On September 30, world-famous aviator Charles A. Lindbergh flew his *Spirit of St. Louis* into Tulsa's first landing strip, McIntyre Airport, on the southeast corner of Admiral Place and Sheridan Road. Lindbergh received a hero's welcome and a parade. Just months earlier, Lindbergh had gained worldwide fame for being the first person to fly nonstop across the Atlantic Ocean from New York to Paris. In Tulsa that day, Lindbergh met another record-setting aviator, Lt. Arthur Goebel, who, weeks before, had been the first to fly across the Pacific Ocean, landing safely in Hawaii. In this McIntyre Airport photograph are, from left to right, Lt. A.C. Strickland (Lindbergh's trainer), Col. Charles A. Lindbergh, Tulsa mayor Herman F. Newblock, and Lt. Arthur Goebel. At the dinner that evening, Lindbergh commented on the small size of McIntyre Airport compared to others in the region. A more suitable facility, Tulsa Municipal Airport, opened the following year. (Courtesy of Beryl Ford Collection/Rotary Club of Tulsa.)

This is an aerial view of Tulsa's Western Village, an ambitious, multimillion-dollar motel/conference center and resort at East Admiral Place and South Garnett Road. Built in the early 1950s by Tulsa developer Roy L. Morgan, the motel had a hexagonal design, while the expansive grounds included a private airstrip, helipad, and an 18-hole golf course that stretched nearly to Eleventh Street, which was Route 66. Opening in 1952 with 33 units, the resort motel expanded to 72 rooms, including 26 cabana suites. The Western motif featured shake roofs, wagon wheels, and wrought-iron decor. Fine dining in the Longhorn Restaurant included pheasant and imported Scottish grouse. That is Admiral Place in the foreground right of the photograph, while the screen of the Highway 66 Drive-In Theatre is visible way in the background. The complex also featured Western-themed retail shops for its guests. (Courtesy of Museum of Tulsa History.)

This postcard peeks inside the hexagon at Western Village into the area of the kidney-shaped pool and cabana. A covered wagon, known in the Sooner State as a schooner, is visible on the right side of the photograph. After several ownership changes and a fire, the sprawling motel/resort property was razed in 1997. (Courtesy of Steve Clem.)

Built in the 1950s after the Mother Road moved to Eleventh Street, Tulsa Auto Court was one of several tourist-oriented businesses constructed on East Admiral Place, along US 75, State Highway 33. Tulsa Auto Court's calling card—its sign—was re-created for Tulsa's Avery Plaza Southwest Neon Park. A historical marker has been placed near where the motel once stood. (Courtesy of Joe Sonderman.)

The iconic Admiral Twin Drive-In Theatre opened in 1951 as the single-screen Modernaire, added a second screen in 1955, and became the Admiral Twin. Still operating in 2025, it is one of the few remaining original outdoor movie experiences on all of Route 66. A 2010 fire destroyed both screens. When the owner announced he did not have the funds to rebuild, it looked like the credits might start rolling "The End." However, the public stepped up to help, and the landmark reopened two years later. The Admiral Twin is also known as a shooting locale for the film *The Outsiders*, shot in Tulsa in 1983. Based on the S.E. Hinton coming-of-age novel, the movie's cast of up-and-comers included Tom Cruise, Patrick Swayze, Matt Dillon, Diane Lane, Ralph Macchio, C. Thomas Howell, and Emilio Estevez. Tulsa's Outsiders House Museum and the award-winning musical *The Outsiders* have rekindled interest in the Admiral Twin's connection to that story. (Courtesy of Beryl Ford Collection/Rotary Club of Tulsa.)

In June 1949, the Sequoia Café at 6004 East Admiral Place advertised complete evening dinners for 95¢ and up and advised Tulsa patrons that "It's Worth Your Time to Drive Out." At that time, the eatery at Admiral Place and Sheridan Road was out in the country. (Courtesy of Mike Ward.)

Formerly known as Shere Court, Seventy-Five Court was named for its location on Highway 75. In its short lifetime from 1946 to 1950, the business changed in 1949 from a tourist court to apartments with weekly rates. It was a next-door neighbor to the Sequoia Café on the south side of Admiral Place at Sheridan Road. (Courtesy of Steve Clem.)

The HI-LO Motel, 6733 East Admiral Place, just east of Sheridan Road, was one of several new motels built along the US Highway 75, State Highway 33 corridor in the years immediately following World War II. Increasingly, the word "motel" was replacing the word "court." The HI-LO's amenities included wall-to-wall carpeting, kitchenettes, tile baths, a pool, and, in the 1950s, free television. (Courtesy of Mike Ward.)

Admiral Courts operated for 25 years. An article in the *Tulsa World* in 1960 relates the story of a traveler who checked into the motel, asking owner Tallef A. Moe if the room had a television set. When the customer had still not returned to the motel late that evening, Moe checked the room and found both the customer and the television gone. (Courtesy of Mike Ward.)

Hank and Ruby Henry opened Hank's Hamburgers on Route 66 at East Eleventh Street and Frisco Avenue, downtown, in 1949. In 1955, Hank's moved to its present location, 8933 East Admiral Place, pictured here. Although other families have taken over, Hank's is still in the conversation for the best old-fashioned hamburgers in Tulsa. (Courtesy of Steve Clem.)

The motto of Anchor Court at 3608 East Admiral Place was "We Deal in Sleep." With its "clean, cool, and comfortable" rooms equipped with cooking facilities, it welcomed travelers from 1946 to the late 1950s, then advertised its cabins for sale to buyers who wanted to start their own motel business or use them for lakeside homes. (Courtesy of Joe Sonderman.)

One of the perks of driving through a city the size of Tulsa, population 182,740 in the 1950 census, was access to entertainment and shopping. Admiral Place became a preferred locale for suburban shopping centers in the 1950s. Three such centers opened during the decade: Eastgate, on the southwest corner at Memorial Drive; Admiral Place Shopping Center, between Harvard Avenue and Yale Avenue; and the largest of the three, Sheridan Village, pictured. Opening in 1954 on the

southwest corner of Admiral Place and Sheridan Road, the two-story complex had the unusual feature of rooftop parking. The ramp is seen on the right of this photograph. Original businesses included J.C. Penney's department store, T.G.&Y. variety store, Humpty Dumpty supermarket, and Oklahoma Tire and Supply (OTASCO). The center also had a Bordens Cafeteria "on the roof terrace." (Courtesy of Museum of Tulsa History.)

Built by Chastain Oil Company for $50,000, the Blue Dome service station opened in January 1925. The Moorish-style building had bays that extended from the dome. The station handled oil changes, lubrication, car washes, and light mechanical work. The 24-hour station could service 12 cars at once. Inside the dome, a spiral staircase led to the manager's small living quarters. The structure also features stone carvings with various motifs. (Courtesy of Steve Rider.)

This view of downtown, from the year Route 66 was created, 1926, shows a delivery truck for Renberg's, one of Tulsa's premier clothiers from 1913 into the 1990s. The Blue Dome on Route 66 is visible, as are the recently completed Philtower and Exchange Bank of Tulsa buildings that gave the Oil Capital its distinctive skyline. (Courtesy of Museum of Tulsa History.)

Countless travelers have partaken in the Tulsa tradition of Ike's Chili. Founded in 1908 by Ike Johnson, four generations of the Johnson family have served this mouth-watering delicacy. The earliest Route 66 motorists could have paused at Ike's 20 West Third Street location, shown here. Mother Road locations have included 5941 Admiral Place and 3208 and 1503 East Eleventh Street. (Courtesy of Museum of Tulsa History.)

A person did not have to own a car to travel Highway 66. Bus lines flourished, and most, including Greyhound, Sante Fe, Trailways, and MK&O, stopped in the Oil Capital. Tulsa's Union Bus Station on the northeast corner of Fourth Street and Cincinnati Avenue, shown in 1934, the year it opened, incorporated elements of Zigzag and Streamline Art Deco. (Courtesy of Beryl Ford Collection/Rotary Club of Tulsa.)

Circle Theatre opened in 1928 on the road's original alignment through Tulsa. The theater's original sign is shown above, while the next phase of the theater's design, its 1940s sign and marquee, is pictured below. Located in the city's first suburban shopping district, Kendall-Whittier, on the corner of East Admiral Place and South Lewis Avenue, the theater featured a Robert Morton pipe organ, which was played to accompany the silent films. When the theater was outfitted for "talkies" around 1930, the organ was sold. During the Circle Cinema Foundation's early-2000s renovation, that original organ was found, repurchased, restored, and is currently in use for the venue's Second Saturday Silent Series. Reopening in 2004, Circle Cinema is Tulsa's only nonprofit historic art house theater as well as the city's oldest movie theater. (Both, courtesy of Oklahoma Historical Society.)

Three

Eleventh Street (1932–1959)

Route 66 Heyday through the Oil Capital

Eleventh Street is considered the classic alignment of the Mother Road through Tulsa—Route 66 for 27 years—through the Great Depression, World War II, and the postwar prosperity of the 1950s.

With Eleventh Street paving completed in 1932, Highway 66 moved one mile south, from Admiral Place to Eleventh Street. This change meant that once a motorist turned from South 193rd East Avenue onto Eleventh Street out in the country east of town, it was a straight shot through the Oil Capital all the way to the Eleventh Street bridge.

Admiral Place remained US 75 and State Highway 33, so tourist services continued to expand there, giving Route 66 travelers additional choices just one mile away.

Unlike the first alignment's path through Tulsa's congested business district, Eleventh Street skimmed the southern edge of downtown past beautiful churches, automobile showrooms, and attractive apartment buildings. Big city shopping and entertainment were just a few blocks away.

In the 1930s, the city ended at Yale Avenue, but new housing additions marched the Magic City steadily east—past Sheridan Road, then Memorial Drive, and beyond. Car dealers, new and used, became a defining characteristic of Eleventh Street, along with the many businesses catering to travelers—gas stations, garages, restaurants, and motor courts—many of them mom-and-pop businesses.

Even the University of Tulsa, which had moved to Eleventh Street in 1904 when it was Henry Kendall College, found its fortunes tied to the economic ups and downs of the Route 66 corridor.

During the Eleventh Street years, each decade brought unique uses for the road—1930s Dust Bowl and Great Depression families traveling west with all their possessions in search of a better life, 1940s troops and supplies during World War II, and the 1950s postwar prosperity that prompted families to "see the USA in their Chevrolet."

The commerce of the nation came down Eleventh Street in Tulsa—the regional salesmen, the long-haul truckers, families visiting relatives, and, in Oklahoma, the illegal commerce of the bootlegger, whose deliveries defied the state's sobering liquor laws. Tulsa's motels, gas stations, and restaurants hosted them all—from check-in to check-out, "check under the hood," and "check, please!"

Retired Tulsa Zoo director Hugh Davis spent two years and hundreds of hours mixing concrete and pouring it over a steel frame for his 80-foot-long, 20-foot-tall whale in Tulsa's eastern suburb of Catoosa. Completed in 1972, adjacent to his Animal Reptile Kingdom (ARK), the concrete giant became a tongue-in-cheek anniversary gift for his wife, Zelta, who chose the whale's color to match her turquoise jewelry. A public swimming hole in the 1970s and 1980s, the new millennium brought restoration to a top attraction on Route 66. (Courtesy of Steve Rider.)

K.V.O. MODERN COURTS
ON U.S. 66-5½ MILES EAST OF TULSA, OKLA.
E.F. SCHMIDT PROPRIETOR
PHONE 6-9979
REASONABLE RATES

CLAREMORE
U.S. 66
17 MILES
K.V.O. MODERN COURTS
HGY #33
TULSA
5 MILES

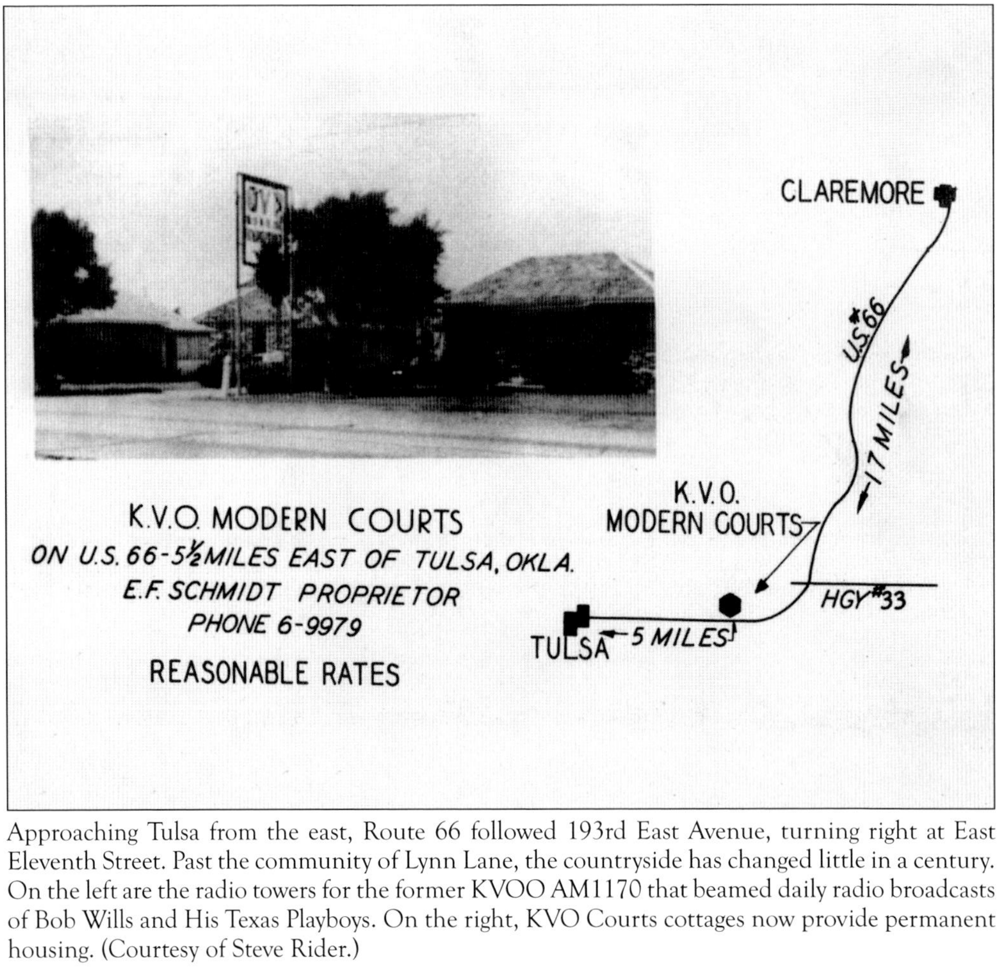

Approaching Tulsa from the east, Route 66 followed 193rd East Avenue, turning right at East Eleventh Street. Past the community of Lynn Lane, the countryside has changed little in a century. On the left are the radio towers for the former KVOO AM1170 that beamed daily radio broadcasts of Bob Wills and His Texas Playboys. On the right, KVO Courts cottages now provide permanent housing. (Courtesy of Steve Rider.)

Two tourist courts east of town, Toby's Beauty-Rest Court and Molder Court, date to the 1940s. They were one block apart on the south side of Eleventh Street, just east of South 129th East Avenue. Toby's wood-framed cabins, arranged in a semicircle, are behind a central office made of rock that was quarried locally. Renting for $3 per night, they had garages and, naturally, Beauty-Rest mattresses. The cottages have been repurposed into apartments, and the office has been extended. Molder Court, below, promised large and airy rooms away from all city and railroad noises. It was demolished. (Above, courtesy of Steve Rider; below, courtesy of Mike Ward.)

The elaborate 1929 tourist complex Pierce Pennant Terminal, east of Garnett Road, closed around World War II. After the war, the 40-room hotel, service station, and café were leased out separately. Frank Bates operated Bates Tourist Hotel, above, from 1945 to 1956. The restaurant became Bing's Café, with this fun advertising postcard, below. In the 1960s, the complex sat abandoned across from East Central High School's stadium and was eventually razed. (Above, courtesy of Joe Sonderman; below, courtesy of Steve Rider.)

This 1940s Tulsa Chamber of Commerce brochure sets the tone for cruisin' Route 66 through the Oil Capital. The top is down, and the couple is enjoying "America's most beautiful city," known for oil, aviation, and the Tulsa Zoo's Monkey Island. The promotional piece concludes with "Tulsa, Oklahoma is ideal for your company's next conference." (Courtesy of Steve Rider.)

This 1960s publicity photograph for Tulsa-refined D-X gasoline was taken at Eleventh Street and Garnett Road. The uniformed service station attendant pumped gas and popped the hood to check the oil. He also served as a cashier, accepting those new forms of payment called credit cards. If a kid was fortunate, like the boy in this photograph, mom and dad might provide a dime for a bottle of "pop," or a "Coke," as Tulsans generically referred to any flavor of soft drink. (Courtesy of Beryl Ford Collection/Tulsa Rotary Club.)

In 1950, Robert Brooks purchased a motel on Route 66 near South Garnett Road that he renamed Brookshire. The attractive court with the white stucco cottage office and large blue neon sign closed in the 2010s and went on the market. While the motel had fallen into disrepair, it was considered a good candidate for restoration. However, two fires dashed those dreams, and the once lovely Brookshire was razed in October 2020. (Courtesy of Steve Clem.)

Oasis Motel, 9303 East Eleventh Street, was built in 1953 near Mingo Road and is still operating. The 30-room motel's swimming pool is now gone, as is the original sign, pictured here. The Oasis's current sign (see page 112) provides a favorite camera click for today's travelers of Historic 66. (Courtesy of Mike Ward.)

The $1 million Saratoga was completed in 1959 at 10117 East Eleventh Street around the time Route 66 moved from Eleventh Street to Interstate 44. This luxury motor hotel featured 85 rooms, conference facilities, a heated pool, a large restaurant, and a private club. The Saratoga rooms' fine furnishings, below, included special amenities like piped-in recorded music and ice water on tap. Expanded to 126 rooms by 1970, travelers ultimately chose the chain motels on the interstate over the Saratoga. In 2024, the nonprofit Wings of Freedom transformed the facility into the Saratoga Sober Living Center. (Above, courtesy of Mike Ward; below, courtesy of Museum of Tulsa History.)

The drive-in theater phenomenon was sweeping the country after World War II, when Tulsa's first outdoor theater, Highway 66 Drive-In, opened in August 1947. On Eleventh Street at South Mingo Road, the theater's advertising helped educate the public on the drive-in experience: "Come as you are . . . eat . . . smoke . . . talk." In this aerial photograph, looking west toward town, Route 66 is on the left. Renamed the Eleventh Street Drive-In and adding a second screen in 1967, the theater operated a few more years but was eventually razed. (Above, courtesy Oklahoma Historical Society; below, courtesy of Steve Rider.)

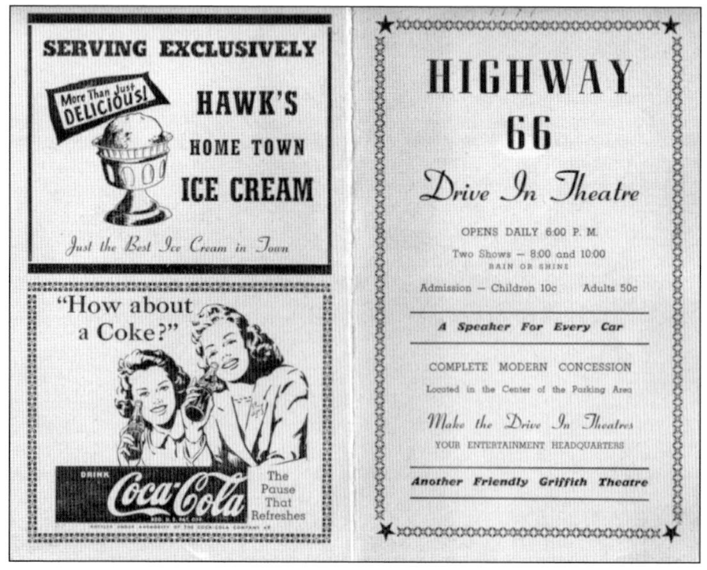

Near the intersection of East Eleventh Street and South Memorial Drive, on the north side of the street, Morris Manor Cottages opened in the 1950s. In 1993, for a *Tulsa World* newspaper article about original Route 66 motels that were still operating, the owner reported that the motor court, pictured here, was on its last legs. No trace of it exists today. (Courtesy of Joe Sonderman.)

US 66 Café was at Tulsa's eastern edge in the 1960s, on Route 66 near South Memorial Drive. Its advertising encouraged travelers to stop for the food as well as the café's "up to date weather and highway information bulletin board." (Courtesy of Mike Ward.)

In 1950, the intersection of East Eleventh Street and South Sheridan Road retained a rural look. Baker's Food Market, to the left, advertised hickory-smoked barbeque, hot chili, and blueberry pie, and the owner, J.C. Baker, also operated a trailer court. On the right, the Glen Haven Cottages, the Cavalier Drive Inn, and the Hickory House Restaurant supplied travelers' needs. (Courtesy of Beryl Ford Collection/Rotary Club of Tulsa.)

In the 1950s, Western themes permeated American culture. In the era of John Wayne movies, Roy Rogers television shows, and kids' cap guns, one could lasso a room at the Western-styled Ranch-O-Tel, Eleventh Street at South Memorial Drive. (Courtesy of Mike Ward.)

The Rose Bowl is one of the more unusual structures on Tulsa's Mother Road. Architect William Henry Ryan's design was based on the concrete bomb shelters he found in Germany during World War I. However, to young bowlers in Tulsa in 1962, the year of *The Jetsons* television cartoon, the bubble-gum pink domes and mid-century furnishings seemed futuristic. Tulsa's One Hope Ministries houses there now. (Courtesy of Museum of Tulsa History.)

During an era when men and women dressed up to go out to dinner, Parkey's Restaurant, near Sheridan Road, invited patrons to "Come as you are." From 1955 to 1970, the eatery with a jukebox selector at every table was the domain of Ike Parkey, who also cofounded the local Silver Castle Diner chain. (Courtesy of Mike Ward.)

In addition to sights, there were smells along Tulsa's Mother Road—the pleasing aroma of fresh-baked bread at Wonder Bread on Eleventh Street at South Sheridan Road, above, and from Rainbo Bread at South Utica Avenue. However, once across the Eleventh Street Bridge, if the wind was just *wrong*, there was the olfactory assault of the oil refineries. (Courtesy of Museum of Tulsa History.)

In 1955, the Leo Trennepohl family moved to Tulsa from Fort Smith to open the Flamingo Motel, 5915 East Eleventh Street. Living in the two-bedroom apartment behind the office, Gary Trennepohl, who was nine years old at the time, recalled helping with room cleanup, taking ice to the rooms, and checking in guests. The Flamingo operates now as Western Motel. (Courtesy of Joe Sonderman.)

The 26-unit Sheridan Hills Motel, just west of Sheridan Road, opened in 1954. It was still in business, 70 years later, with a name change to Super 11 Inn. The motel's heated swimming pool, pictured, helped travelers relax after a long day on the road. (Courtesy of Mike Ward.)

In 1933, real estate operators B.L. O'Connor and A.J. Sheffield established the National Camp-O-Tel Association with Tulsa as its headquarters. Their mission was to designate "high class tourist camps" every 50 to 100 miles along the nation's highways, marking the camps/motels with a blinker atop a lighthouse structure. Cook's Court, 5900 East Eleventh Street, was the first so designated by the short-lived association. (Courtesy of Steve Clem.)

This c. 1960 eastern view down Eleventh Street between Yale Avenue and Sheridan Road reveals a concentration of classic motels. Vintage neon signs are visible for Grotto Courts, Tulsa Mo-Tel, and, in the distance, Will Rogers Motor Court. Signage for McCollum's Restaurant, Ashby's Café, and Pizza King are also seen. (Courtesy of Museum of Tulsa History.)

This postcard from the road, composed at the Grotto, was bound for Santiago, California, as the traveler headed east. Postmarked May 7, 1958, the writer recounts the driving day just past—"cool temperatures and high speeds of 70 miles per hour on the divided highway of the Turner Turnpike." Notice the arrow, carved into the postcard's left side, indicating the cottage the sender stayed in. (Courtesy of Mike Ward.)

The newspaper advertisement referred to it as "America's Finest Motor Court." However, when Paul and Dora Johnson purchased Will Rogers Motor Court in 1946, they would make it even better. Their son Paul started managing the property the following year. Four years later, the motor court added its iconic lassoing cowboy neon sign. With "36 ultra-modern 2-room units," a pool was added in 1958. The office switchboard could connect guests to McCollum's Restaurant next door, which provided room service. While the motel is gone, its spectacular neon sign has been replicated in Avery Plaza Southwest neon sign park. (Above, courtesy of Joe Sonderman; right, courtesy of John Marguiles/ Library of Congress.)

The word "motel" was just coming into the language when Mr. and Mrs. Don D. Parker of Amarillo purchased Tulsa Mo-Tel, 5715 East Eleventh Street, in May 1944. Positioned in the cluster of motor courts between Yale Avenue and Sheridan Road, over time, many other "courts" would change their name to "motel." Notice the Mo-Tel's cool space-age sign. (Courtesy of Steve Clem.)

Tulsan Herman H. Whitt built his first tourist court at 3608 East Admiral Place on Highway 66's early alignment. After the highway was rerouted to Eleventh Street in the 1930s, Whitt constructed the 36-unit Whitt's Motel at 5318 East Eleventh Street. Whitt, a former state director of the US 66 Highway Association, died in the late 1950s, after which the court operated as Bel-Air Motel. (Courtesy of Museum of Tulsa History.)

Tulsan Robert S. Mitchell and Glenn Bennett of Oklahoma City built the Flamingo Motel and the Desert Hills Motel. Opening in 1953, the Desert Hills catered to traveling salesmen and families. Current owner Jack Patel has remodeled the rooms and maintained the spectacular neon sign to provide today's travelers with a classic motel experience. The neon of Whitt's Motel is visible in the background of this 1950s image. (Courtesy of Mike Ward.)

While so many businesses that catered to Route 66 travelers through Tulsa are gone, the memories, and a few remnants, remain: from Will Rogers Motor Court, a room key (No. 20) and a logoed bar of soap; matches from McCollum's Restaurant and Saratoga Motel; and matchbook covers from the Flamingo Motel and Parkey's Restaurant. (Courtesy of Steve Clem.)

This bird's-eye view, taken from atop the Safeway store at Eleventh Street and Yale Avenue, shows the mobile nature of American life around 1955. At least three service stations are visible: on the left, Q's Service Station with a sign advertising D-X fuel; on the right, Hudson Filling Station and Creekmore Texaco as well as its next-door neighbor, Tulsa Trailerhomes. (Courtesy of Beryl Ford Collection/Rotary Club of Tulsa.)

The Golden Drumstick, northeast corner of Eleventh Street and Yale Avenue, had something for the whole family—delicious fried chicken and a wishing well where a child could win a toy. Opened in 1948 by Bill and Bob Latting, it became the Middle Path restaurant in the 1970s. A convenience store and a handful of interpretive panels about Tulsa Route 66 occupy this corner today. (Courtesy of Mike Ward.)

If someone throws a rock in this part of Oklahoma, it is likely to hit something named for Oklahoma's beloved native son, Will Rogers. In fact, the entire Mother Road is dedicated to the early-20th-century entertainer. At right, Will Rogers Theatre, built in 1941 at 4500 East Eleventh Street, had a Streamline Moderne Art Deco marquee and tower. A Southwest motif graced the inside. The movie house was frequented by students from nearby Will Rogers High School, including Gailard Sartain, who became a successful character actor and artist. The school, with a striking Art Deco design, is still open, while the theater, purchased by a local church, was demolished. (Right, courtesy of Museum of Tulsa History; below, courtesy of Mike Ward.)

Wolf Robe's Indian Trading Post was on the northeast corner of Eleventh Street at Harvard Avenue. Native American artist Wayne Henry "Wolf Robe" Hunt was known for his silversmithing and turquoise jewelry. A member of the Acoma tribe, his store carried Acoma pottery, Osage beadwork, and Navajo jewelry. In 1952, Hunt relocated to Catoosa, across from the ARK (Animal Reptile Kingdom). This building was demolished. (Courtesy of Museum of Tulsa History.)

The Casa Loma Hotel, 2630 East Eleventh Street, predates Eleventh Street's designation as Route 66. Built in 1927 by Max Campbell, the impressive, block-long Spanish Mission structure featured retail spaces on the first floor and hotel rooms with in-room baths above. Added to the National Register of Historic Places in 2010, the following year, the remodeled property reopened as the Campbell Hotel. (Courtesy of Beryl Ford Collection/Rotary Club of Tulsa.)

This c. 1950 photograph shows the buildings across the street from the Casa Loma Hotel. The Royal Theatre, which operated from 1948 to 1957, was one of a half dozen movie houses a Route 66 traveler through Tulsa would have encountered during the road's heyday. In 1957, it became Danceland. Bama Pie offices and parking occupy this block now. (Courtesy of Museum of Tulsa History.)

In September 1948, during the US presidential election campaign, Pres. Harry S. Truman came to Tulsa by train on a whistle-stop tour. He proceeded by car from the Mayo Hotel on Route 66 to the University of Tulsa's Skelly Stadium, where he delivered a speech to a crowd of 20,000. The president urged support for Democratic candidates in the upcoming November election. (Courtesy of Museum of Tulsa History.)

Founded by Alabama "Bama" Marshall in her kitchen in Texas in 1927, Bama Pie came to Tulsa when Marshall's son Paul moved here in 1937. This 1943 photograph shows employees posing at the company's building on East Eleventh Street and South Delaware Avenue. The company began producing pies for McDonald's in 1967; anyone who has had a McDonald's turnover has had a Bama Pie. (Courtesy of Beryl Ford Collection/Rotary Club of Tulsa.)

What began as the Presbyterian School for Indian Girls in Muskogee was chartered as Henry Kendall College before becoming the University of Tulsa in 1920. In 1966, record enrollment resulted in a student housing shortage. The owner of Downtown Motel, three blocks from campus on East Eleventh Street, gifted the 70-unit, $300,000 motel to the university for use as additional student housing. (Courtesy of Mike Ward.)

Miss Tulsa Lunch, in a former Silver Castle Diner on Eleventh Street near Utica Avenue, was operated by Dale McCollum, whose uncle had been a partner in the Silver Castle chain. After a 1958 fire closed Miss Tulsa Lunch, McCollum bought a restaurant three miles east that was located between two Route 66 motels, Will Rogers Motor Court and Tulsa Mo-Tel. He renamed it McCollum's. (Courtesy of Museum of Tulsa History.)

Leroy and Richard Borden opened their first restaurant in downtown Tulsa in 1935, eventually operating several in different areas of the city, each with their own decor. The exterior at Eleventh Street and South Birmingham Place had modern lines, octagonal windows, and a neon sign advertising popular restaurant food choices. The last Bordens in Tulsa closed in 1989. (Courtesy of Museum of Tulsa History.)

This commercial building on East Eleventh Street at South Xanthus Avenue was designed by Bruce Goff for Guaranty Laundry in 1928. A fur storage addition was completed in 1940. In 1976, W.S. Page purchased the property for his family-owned moving company, Page Storage and Van Lines, one of the city's longest-running family businesses, since 1910. (Courtesy of Lyman Page.)

On their 40th anniversary in business, the owners of Tulsa Monument Company moved from downtown to Eleventh Street and Victor Avenue, where there was room for their building materials and easy access to Route 66 for deliveries. The architect of the new building, Harry H. Mahler, designed it to look like a monument in an Art Deco style known as "three-bar modern." (Courtesy Museum of Tulsa History.)

California restaurateur Bob Wian sliced a hamburger bun into three portions and added two meat patties in between, his own special sauce, and condiments. Bob's Big Boy was born. When Wian let franchisees use their own name, Kip's Big Boy served Kansas, Oklahoma, and Texas. This location, near Hillcrest Hospital, became a late-night favorite for University of Tulsa students. (Courtesy of Beryl Ford Collection/Rotary Club of Tulsa.)

An unidentified man enters Cecil's Dinner House, 1611 East Eleventh Street, one of the nearly 40 restaurant choices on the route through Tulsa in the early 1960s. Others included Sandy's Drive-In, Pancho's Mexican, and, serving the new cuisine sweeping the nation, Pizza Parlor, later rebranded as Ken's Pizza. (Courtesy of Beryl Ford Collection/Rotary Club of Tulsa.)

In 1959, after Route 66 moved to Interstate 44, Eleventh Street was signed "Business 66." This c. 1960 photograph looking east from Peoria shows Meek's Furniture, Brinlee's Thrif-T-Wise, and, across the street, the Studebaker car dealership and PEMCO Service station. This busy block is now home to Meadow Gold Mack, the Meadow Gold sign, and Buck Atom's Cosmic Curios. (Courtesy of Beryl Ford Collection/Rotary Club of Tulsa.)

Looking west from east of Peoria Avenue, this view of Eleventh Street from the late 1940s shows longtime Tulsa businesses, Meek's Furniture (left, now the location of Wildflower Café) and Knapp Advertising, supplier of billboards. Other businesses are Buy-Right Grocery Store and Monty's Bar on the left, with White House Café and Brilliant Bronze Service Station on the right. (Courtesy of Beryl Ford Collection/Rotary Club of Tulsa.)

This 1940s image shows the Public Market complex, completed in 1930 on the former site of McNulty Park at East Tenth Street and South Elgin Avenue. Architect B. Gaylord Noftsger's design featured a tall tower, colorful Art Deco terra-cotta, and tile embellishments. Warehouse Market occupied the building from 1938 to 1978. A 1994 renovation by Home Depot saved the landmark from demolition. (Courtesy of Beryl Ford Collection/Rotary Club of Tulsa.)

In the mid-1950s, at Chuc-Wagun, on Eleventh Street between Utica Avenue and Lewis Avenue, Wheel Burgers and Hub Burgers ruled the day. This 1957 photograph looks east, capturing a Route 66 shield, American Furniture, and the historic Guaranty Laundry building, home of Page Storage and Van Lines since the 1970s. (Courtesy of Museum of Tulsa History.)

National recording artists Chuck Berry and Jerry Lee Lewis both performed around 1960 at KAKC Radio AM970's teen "sock hops" at Continental Skating Rink, above, just west of Tracy Park. Lewis's reputation for breaking pianos preceded him, but he promised KAKC program director Dick Schmitz that he would not damage the rented piano that night. Lewis kept his word. (Courtesy of Museum of Tulsa History.)

This 1940s aerial photograph of South Boston Avenue looking south from Tenth Street reveals the octagonal building that had been Bishop's Driv-Inn restaurant, Greenlease-Ledterman Cadillac, and, across Eleventh Street, Horace Mann Jr. High. The crown jewel of Tulsa Art Deco architecture, Boston Avenue United Methodist Church, sits majestically in the background. (Courtesy of Museum of Tulsa History.)

Here is a closer look at what is considered one of the finest examples of ecclesiastical architecture in the United States. Boston Avenue United Methodist Church, the striking Art Deco structure with a 225-foot tower, was designed by Adah Robinson and Bruce Goff. The National Park Service has designated the 1929 building a national historic landmark. (Courtesy of Mike Ward.)

One of the more unusual overnight choices for travelers was tucked away one block off the route at Twelfth Street and Cheyenne Avenue. Cheyenne Arms, which combined a four-story apartment building with a small, ground-level motel, was a cozy spot in the city that was close to downtown shopping. (Courtesy of Joe Sonderman.)

William W. Bishop's sit-down restaurant in the business district was already a success when he opened Bishop's Driv-Inn at downtown's edge, one block off Route 66, in 1936. Bishop's octagonal design, influenced by the circular carhop eateries in Southern California, offered carhop service and indoor dining. The restaurant closed during the gas rationing of World War II. The building was later razed. (Courtesy of Museum of Tulsa History.)

What was once the location of the Ranch House Café at 807 West Eleventh Street is now obscured in the confluence of highways near the Oklahoma State University Medical Center and not far from the Cyrus Avery Centennial Plaza. An advertisement in *Tulsa County News* in 1960 suggested the eight-ounce T-bone steak for $1 and "always 5¢" coffee. (Courtesy of Mike Ward.)

Here are two opposite views from around 1952 of one of the busiest intersections in Tulsa, Eleventh Street and Denver Avenue, the crossroads of US 66 and US 64/SH 51. Above, looking west, Crown Drug is on the northwest corner, while Safeway occupies the southwest corner. Bowen Lounge, the filming location for the opening scene of the 1983 movie *The Outsiders*, is on the southeast corner. Below, looking east, the Tower Theatre advertises *My Man Godfrey* as pedestrians cross at the light. The Lorraine Apartments are on the northeast corner. Retail businesses Simmons Shoe Rebuilders and La Scala Restaurant are visible in the background, along with two churches that flank Route 66 at Boulder Avenue. While these church buildings survive, none of the structures at this once busy intersection exist today. (Both, courtesy of Beryl Ford Collection/Rotary Club of Tulsa.)

All through the years, the US 66 Highway Association published brochures touting the route as the best way west. This vintage 1950s promotional piece brands the route as the Will Rogers Highway and the Grand Canyon Route as well as promoting all the miles of four-lane highway on the modern-day Mother Road. Inside, there is a map of the entire route with illustrated highlights of attractions along the way. (Courtesy of Steve Clem.)

Four

Quanah Avenue/ Southwest Boulevard (1926–1959)

Westside Pride

After crossing the Eleventh Street bridge, Route 66 entered the west side of Tulsa. While this entire area of town is often called West Tulsa, that name refers to a specific area just west of the river that was incorporated as a town in 1907 and annexed to the City of Tulsa in 1909. West Tulsa's business district, of which there is no trace today, thrived during much of the Route 66 years of 1926 to 1959.

The Westside is an amalgamation of communities that were once incorporated towns; in addition to West Tulsa, other towns included Red Fork (incorporated in 1902, annexed to Tulsa in 1927), Garden City (incorporated 1924, annexed 1950), and Carbondale (incorporated 1925, annexed 1928) as well as the communities of Berryhill, Oakhurst, and South Haven. Even today, a resident of Garden City, Red Fork, or Berryhill would be more likely to say that they live in that community, rather than Tulsa or even West Tulsa.

The story of Route 66 in Tulsa began in Red Fork in 1901 when the Sue A. Bland No. 1 oil well came in. Oilmen flocked to the area and built the refineries and businesses that made Tulsa the "Oil Capital of the World" and still fuel much of the business and philanthropic effort in the city. The needs of the oil companies built the bridge, and the bridge made Tulsa's Route 66 possible.

The numerous tourist courts were the "welcome wagon" for motorists entering Tulsa from the west. Heavy traffic on the route was an often-visited topic for Westsiders. An Oklahoma Department of Transportation (ODOT) widening project expanded Route 66 on the west side to four lanes in 1949.

The three-mile route passed oil refineries, railroad yards, tank farms, and, just past the business district of Red Fork, Crystal City Amusement Park. With picnic grounds, a giant swimming pool, amusement rides, and Casa Loma dance hall, the park's years of operation approximated the Westside's years as Route 66.

In 1957, Quanah Avenue and Sapulpa Road were combined into one long thoroughfare, Southwest Boulevard, which helped to make the Westside a unified whole. The photographs in this chapter depict locations along the route from east to west.

This aerial photograph looking at the downtown Tulsa skyline from above the Frisco Railway yard in West Tulsa could hardly be a more perfect example of what has made the Westside what it is. It is the historic home of blue-collar workers in transportation and industry, which is separated from Tulsa proper by a river, joined to it by a bridge, and shaped by the road that runs through it. (Courtesy of Robert "Bob" McCormack Collection, McFarlin Library, University of Tulsa, and Museum of Tulsa History.)

After crossing the Eleventh Street Bridge into West Tulsa in 1952 (the date of this photograph), travelers would take Route 66, the wide road to the left, known locally as Quanah Avenue. The branching road to the right, Rosedale Avenue, would take workers to their refinery jobs. In the distance to the south, West Tulsa's business district is just visible. (Courtesy of the Southwest Tulsa Historical Society.)

Quanah Avenue between Seventeenth and Nineteenth Streets was a thriving shopping district with a Safeway grocery store, hotels, cafés, small businesses, a movie theater, and an Oklahoma Tire and Supply. This photograph was taken before the name of the street was changed to Southwest Boulevard in 1957. Due to an urban renewal project in the 1970s, none of these buildings remain. (Courtesy of Beryl Ford Collection/Rotary Club of Tulsa.)

Quanah Avenue was already a busy, mixed-use thoroughfare when these photographs were taken around 1930. On Quanah Avenue at Twenty-Third Street (above), residences mixed with businesses such the furniture store on the left and the barbershop on the right that served a local clientele. On Quanah Avenue at Twenty-Fourth Street (below), residences were giving way to service stations, like the Barnsdall Refining Company station, and diners, like S.F. Emrich's restaurant, which catered to the needs of travelers on Route 66 as well as railroad and refinery workers. On the right, the trees indicate the location of Howard Park, while on the left, the first of a solid mile of oil storage tanks stretches from Twenty-Fifth Street to Thirty-Fifth Street along Sapulpa Road/Route 66. (Above, courtesy of Southwest Tulsa Historical Society; below, courtesy of Beryl Ford Collection/Rotary Club of Tulsa.)

This 1967 image looks east toward Southwest Boulevard from the Twenty-Third Street overpass. The highway sign at center right reads 75, 33, and Business 66. In 2025, Ed's Hamburgers has been replaced by a McDonald's, while QuikTrip convenience store occupies the spot of Sutterfield's DX service station. (Courtesy of Museum of Tulsa History.)

Rio Courts opened around 1940 on the southeast corner of Quanah Avenue at West Twenty-Third Street. Owner Porter Albee and manager J.M. Baker were active in projects to promote Route 66 tourism. In 1941, Baker was elected state president for Oklahoma at the US 66 Highway Association's convention in Tucumcari. The contents of the motel were sold at an urban renewal auction in September 1967. (Courtesy of Joe Sonderman.)

SILVER CASTLE NO. 13 – WEST TULSA, OKLAHOMA

Business partners Ike Parkey and James McCollum founded the Silver Castle restaurant chain in Tulsa in 1936. Inspired by the White Castle chain, the Silver Castle Lunch System, as it was called, featured chrome and porcelain in an Art Deco style on the exterior of the restaurants and vinyl-covered booths and a lunch counter with stools in the interior. The partners built nine restaurants in Tulsa, three of them on Route 66, and expanded into Kansas, Missouri, and Texas. Silver Castle No. 13 was located at 2341 Southwest Boulevard. Tulsa restaurant-owner Claud Hobson ran No. 13 before opening his own restaurant, Claud's, on South Peoria Avenue in 1954. (Both, courtesy of Steve Rider.)

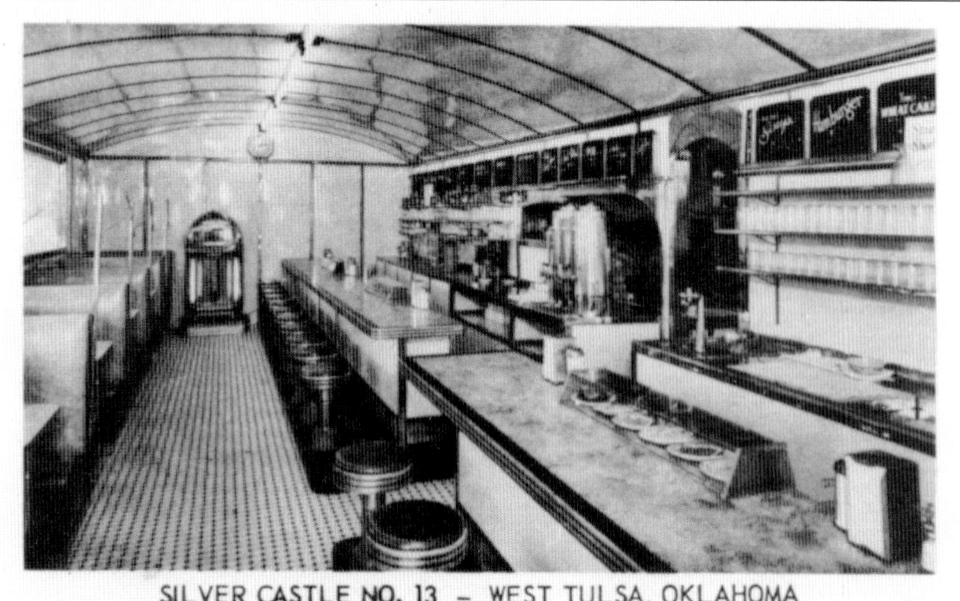

SILVER CASTLE NO. 13 – WEST TULSA, OKLAHOMA

Embracing the benefits of a location on Route 66, Chicken 66 sold fried chicken in a box for 66¢. Travelers in a hurry could even order it to go. (Courtesy of Mike Ward.)

Likewise, owner Dick Love's D&D Barbecue offered hickory-smoked meats with drive-in curb service. He also advertised Hi-Spot, a carbonated lemon drink sold by Canada Dry. (Courtesy of Steve Rider.)

Above, in 1950, commercial establishments abound on this recently widened stretch of Route 66. Art's Tydol and Montgomery and Jacobsen Texaco face each other across the highway. The Tidewater Oil Company began selling products with the Tydol brand in the 1920s. Flying A later became the company's main brand. In 1966, Phillips Petroleum Company bought out Tidewater's western holdings and changed all the Flying A stations to Phillips 66. Texaco began in Beaumont in 1902 as the Texas Company. The Texaco star became its logo in 1903 when a refinery worker suggested using the five-pointed symbol of Texas, later adding the green "T." After nearly a century, the Texaco brand was retired in Oklahoma in 2001. (Both, courtesy of the Oklahoma Department of Transportation Collection, Oklahoma Historical Society.)

As Route 66 moves through the Westside from Twenty-Fifth Street to Thirty-Sixth Street, a refinery and tank farm borders it on the east, and a vast railroad facility borders it on the west. On the southern end of the tank farm (above) at Thirty-Sixth Street is Garden City, which began when town lots for homes were sold to Texaco Company refinery employees in the 1910s. The 1940s image above shows the route signed as 66 and 75 and Highway 169. Moving through time 25 years, in the 1970 photograph of the railyard at right, a sign names the facility as Cherokee Yard, which is now one of eight BNSF (Burlington Northern Santa Fe) classification yards used to sort incoming cars and "build" outgoing segments of railcars. (Above, Oklahoma Department of Transportation Collection, Oklahoma Historical Society; right, Barriger Railroad Library, St. Louis Mercantile Library.)

The Pig in Pen restaurant and Toby's Truck Stop offered services to travelers on Route 66 from their location in the 3500 block of Sapulpa Road near Park Plaza Courts. Johney Harden, who worked at Pig in Pen as well as Silver Castle, later owned the first Kentucky Fried Chicken franchise in Tulsa and founded Harden's Hamburgers. (Courtesy of Southwest Tulsa Historical Society.)

In 1961, this Texaco station at 3556 Southwest Boulevard sold its Fire Chief brand of gasoline for 24¢ a gallon and its Sky Chief brand for 29¢ a gallon, while offering S&H Green Stamps as an incentive to customers. Texaco's "Trust your car to the man who wears the star" advertising campaign would come along in 1962. (Courtesy of Southwest Tulsa Historical Society.)

Brothers Milton and Lemuel Stroud built Park Plaza Courts in Tulsa in 1942 at 3512 Sapulpa Road. Based on the Alamo Courts chain, they placed their Spanish-style motel with kitchenettes at one-day driving intervals—St. Louis, Tulsa, Amarillo, and Flagstaff on Route 66—so travelers could stay in a Park Plaza Courts every night. In the 1980s, owner Dorothy Harrison provided housing for the homeless and other marginalized individuals at the classic motel. However, after financing failed and maintenance lapsed, the building was razed in 1988. Below, the ODOT image shows the curve with Park Plaza Courts before the 1949 widening project. Since 1984, Billy Ray's Catfish and Barbeque has occupied a space on that curve. (Above, courtesy of Steve Clem; below, courtesy of Oklahoma Historical Society.)

In Act I, in 1933, Isaac Burnaman built 17 concrete block units covered with stucco at 3660 Sapulpa Road. He named the cabins with attached garages El Reposo, "place of rest." The complex had a café and filling station but was reduced in size with the 1949 widening of Westside 66. (Courtesy of Steve Clem.)

Act II of the property at 3660 Sapulpa Road involved a name change to Western Motel from 1960 to 1964. In this photograph, looking west along Route 66 at Union Avenue, the Western sign is seen. There would be another name change and nostalgia for this classic court in Act III, which also reveals whether the story is a comedy or a tragedy. (Courtesy of Museum of Tulsa History.)

In Act III, Ken and Noma Undernehr purchased the property now called 66 Motel in 1967. Business 66 still provided plenty of guests. The couple remade some rooms into living quarters, leaving 11 guest rooms. The court was listed in the National Register of Historic Places in 1996. Vandalism and the property's deteriorating condition contributed to its demolition in 2001. It was a tragedy. (Courtesy of Museum of Tulsa History.)

Visible from Route 66, Daniel Webster High School was completed in 1938 by the Public Works Administration (PWA). In addition to being known for its Art Deco architecture and college-like campus, Webster is also recognized as being the first Tulsa high school to be integrated, in 1955. It was added to the National Register of Historic Places in 2021. (Courtesy of Robert "Bob" McCormack Collection, McFarlin Library, University of Tulsa.)

In 1936, Tulsa plumbing inspector Maurice Colpitts built 13 modest cottages at 3848 Sapulpa Road. The 10-by-12-foot bungalows closely matched plans published in *Popular Mechanics* magazine the previous year. There was just enough room for two people and a full-sized bed, and by the 1990s, the court's reputation matched its "shady" name. In an article entitled "Even the losers need a place to sleep" on the *Route 66 News* website, author Ron Warnick references a book that describes Shady Rest as a place where "folks . . . claw and hang on by their fingernails." The dilapidated tourist court's 70 years of history on Route 66 was not enough to save it from the bulldozers after it was cited for code infractions by city inspectors and ordered to vacate in 2005. (Above, courtesy of Mike Ward; left, courtesy of Museum of Tulsa History.)

For over a decade in the 1950s and 1960s, the Quality Gas Station at 3722 Southwest Boulevard provided inexpensive gas and a place for Westside kids to fold morning newspapers before heading out on their paper routes. When the long-vacant building was demolished in 2013, the Bell oil products sign was saved and now lives at the Route 66 Historical Village. (Courtesy of the Oklahoma Historical Society.)

Westside doctors Fred S. Clinton and John C.W. Bland were instrumental in the drilling of the Sue A. Bland No. 1 well, named for Dr. Bland's wife, on whose Muscogee Creek allotment the well was located. The well came in on June 24, 1901, generating construction of the first Westside refineries and creating the need for a bridge across the Arkansas River. (Courtesy of Museum of Tulsa History.)

This photograph, a "before" example from an Oklahoma Department of Transportation widening project, shows the intersection of Forty-First Street and Southwest Boulevard, well-known to current citizens of Red Fork, even though few features remain that were present in 1949. The two-story Cove Apartments, center right, once housed Dooley Drug, a Westside pharmacy with a long history, on its bottom floor. (Courtesy of Oklahoma Department of Transportation Collection, Oklahoma Historical Society.)

The Cove Theater, located across West Forty-First Street from the Cove Apartments, appears here on a February night in 1947. The marquee advertises *The Daltons Ride Again,* a 1945 film that starred Lon Chaney Jr., who was born in Oklahoma City; Noah Beery Jr.; and Milburn Stone, who later played Doc on *Gunsmoke*. Neither the apartment building nor the theater exists today. (Courtesy of Murrel Wilmoth.)

This photograph captures the southwest corner of Southwest Boulevard and South Twenty-Sixth West Avenue and looks across the highway to the Safeway grocery store, which stood in the approximate location where Ollie's Station restaurant stands today. At the corner of a row of businesses, Red Fork Drug, better known as Brownie's, sold everything from medicine to comic books to Glencliff ice cream. (Courtesy of Museum of Tulsa History.)

After starting a chain of grocery stores in Oregon in the 1920s, M.B. Skaggs merged his stores with another chain and renamed it Safeway. Since the groceries did not offer credit or create debt, it was the "safe way" to buy food. Safeway had stores in both West Tulsa and Red Fork; this one later moved to the Crystal City Shopping Center. (Courtesy of Museum of Tulsa History.)

This row of century-old buildings is about all that remains of Red Fork's old business district. Platted as the Galbreath Colcord Russell Addition to the Town of Red Fork, it housed Whitener's Department Store, Red Fork Drug, Hopkins Dry Goods, and the El Dorado Bar in the 1950s. The Tulsa Stove Hospital and the Red Fork Art Gallery are current occupants of the buildings. (Courtesy of Oklahoma Department of Transportation.)

In 1964, Ike Wall celebrated the grand opening of his DX service station next door to the Safeway store. Just visible in the background is the same row of buildings shown in the previous photograph, across Route 66/Southwest Boulevard from the new station. (Courtesy of Joy Ryker.)

Opening in 1928, Crystal City Amusement Park was an early attraction on Route 66. In addition to a roller coaster named Zingo, a midway with rides, a miniature railroad, a swimming pool, a lagoon, and picnic grounds, the park also featured a dance pavilion called Casa Loma, where couples could dance the night away to the music of Bob Wills and His Texas Playboys. (Courtesy of Museum of Tulsa History.)

In 1960, Crystal City Shopping Center replaced the amusement park. Westsiders have supported its groceries, pharmacies, department stores, and restaurants for decades. Recently, Arnold's Old-Fashioned Hamburgers, a popular 1950s-style diner, has thrived at its Crystal City location. In this photograph, local radio/television personality Jack Morris interviews Mayor James Maxwell in front of Crawford's Drug, the centerpiece of the shopping center in the 1960s. (Courtesy of Museum of Tulsa History.)

Above, Ike Wall's father, Frank, stands in front of his son's service station at Thirty-Third West Avenue and Southwest Boulevard in 1956. This little building has had nine lives—as several auto-related businesses, as a diner featuring grilled cheese sandwiches, and as an insurance agency. (Courtesy of Joy Ryker.)

Leaving Tulsa, for many travelers, the next stop was the Frankoma Pottery factory store in Sapulpa. Ceramic artist John Frank opened Frankoma on Sapulpa Route 66 in 1938. Its dinnerware lines, political mugs, Christmas plates, figurines, and sculptures influenced mid-century pottery design. Although the plant closed in 2010, Frankoma Pottery—fired from regional clays in glazes, including prairie green and desert gold—is still collected worldwide. (Courtesy of Steve Rider.)

Five

66 Bypass/Skelly Bypass/ Interstate 44

Chain Motels and Check-out Time for Mom and Pop

After delays and a $15 million price tag, Interstate 44 opened on the southern outskirts of Tulsa in November 1958. Route 66 moved over to Interstate 44 a few months later, leaving the Eleventh Street/Southwest Boulevard route to be designated as "Business 66."

Initially known as 66 Bypass, the new four-lane thoroughfare was officially named Skelly Bypass, honoring Tulsa oilman and philanthropist William G. Skelly. One of Skelly's early accomplishments was teaming with Cyrus Avery on building the Tulsa Municipal Airport in 1928.

I-44 brought high-speed travel and new motels, with several clustered near the Turner Turnpike entrance in southwest Tulsa.

From the Turner gate, traveling west to east, Interstate 44 followed East Fifty-First Street to around Yale Avenue, then veered northeast, connecting to the Will Rogers Turnpike east of town.

The contrast between the interstate highway and the road it replaced, Route 66, could not be more dramatic. "Bypass" was the correct word. On the elevated interstate, travelers bypassed America. The only stops were when motorists dipped down onto an exit to visit chain restaurants, gas stations, and motels identical in appearance and function to the establishments they encountered the previous day and would patronize tomorrow. Route 66 traversed the heart of the nation's towns and cities, hugging the terrain.

The opening of I-44 through Tulsa brought the super-sized "motor hotel," with 200 or more large rooms, bigger swimming pools, roomier restaurants, and convention facilities. Many featured a playground for kids as well as one for adults in the form of a lounge or club.

At first, the mom-and-pop motels along Eleventh Street/Southwest Boulevard reported only a slight reduction in occupancy. However, the 1960s changed that. Tulsa's populations shifted south to the suburbs, and commerce followed. Two new shopping centers at Forty-First Street and Yale Avenue caused downtown shopping to dry up almost overnight. By decade's end, Tulsa's historic routes through the city had begun their steady, prolonged declines.

Interstate 44 opened in late 1958 and carried the traffic of Route 66 a few months later. Interstate 44/66 Bypass/Skelly Bypass connected the Turner Turnpike at Tulsa's western limits to the Will Rogers Turnpike east of town. Westbound travelers approaching the Turner gate could choose between the toll road or the "free road" between Tulsa and Sapulpa, completed in 1951, which paralleled the turnpike to the east. (Courtesy of Steve Clem.)

On a 1951 vacation, after a motel charged him an extra $2 for each of his five children, Memphian Kemmons Wilson decided to build a chain of motels that would never charge for children staying in the same room as their parents. Tulsa's first Holiday Inn, near the Turner Turnpike gate, opened in 1959, operated by husband-and-wife team Charles E. and Phyrne McCracken. (Courtesy of Joe Sonderman.)

New

Winston MOTOR COURT

AND RESTAURANT

TULSA, OKLAHOMA

Fine Food at moderate prices (Room Service)

Large, Charming

POOL and PATIO

for your fun and relaxation

Kiddies pool and playground for the little ones.

Free ice and baby needs.

Twenty-four hour telephone service.

Beautiful lobby.

Laundry and dry cleaning service.

Newspapers and magazines.

INSTON'S is ideally located for
e business man and the traveler.

ELAX IN LUXURY

66 Quiet and Delightful Roo

Year-'round central heating and re
erated cooling.

Spacious one and two room units
lovely baths with tubs and shov

Free television in each room.

There is more than just comfort .
there's charm and color in every rc

West edge of Tulsa on Interstate 44, U.S. 66, U.S. 75, State 33, on By-pass near the Turnpike entrance

For Reservations

Telephone HIckory 6-6137 . . . or write to Winston Motor Court, 5609 New Sapulpa Rd., Tulsa, Oklahoma

Rates are reasonable! Come . . . see for yourself that the best costs no more. You're always welcome at Winston's

You'll Always Remember The Luxurious Accommodations at Winston MOTOR COURT

This c. 1970 brochure advertises Winston's Motor Court, 5609 West Skelly Drive, northeast of the turnpike gate. Opening in the 1950s with 23 rooms, two additional wings expanded the one-story motel to 66 rooms. This advertisement does a masterful job of masking the fact that the Winston was a smaller, no-frills motel competing with newer, super-sized chain motels with their 200 luxury rooms, heated swimming pools, fine dining, and on-site lounges. It must have worked! The Winston was still in business 70 years later, making it one of the longest continuously operating motels along Tulsa's Interstate 44. (Courtesy of Rhys Martin.)

When a cluster of new motels opened with Interstate 44, overnight Tulsa went from a shortage of motel rooms to having too many to fill. Occupancy rates slowly increased with more traffic in the early 1960s. Town and Country, in the middle of the motels near the Turner Turnpike entrance, catered to vacationing families and businessmen with two- and three-bedroom suites. (Courtesy of Steve Clem.)

Three of the new motels near the Turner Turnpike gate were built and then sold by Tulsan Robert S. Mitchell—the Sands, Town and Country, and Western Capri. The Sands and Western Capri both had large mid-century modern neon signs with an arrow to attract customers. Like most motels of that era, the eye-catching neon was eventually replaced by inexpensive, aesthetically uninteresting signage. (Courtesy of Mike Ward.)

Not all motels on Interstate 44 were profitable, so some owners considered alternate revenue streams. In 1970, the Sands, at the Tulsa County/Creek County border, leased the 64-room motel to the State of Oklahoma for a proposed prison prerelease center, mirroring its Oklahoma City halfway house. However, after nearby residents and motel owners mounted stiff opposition, the state announced the plan would not move forward. (Courtesy of Mike Ward.)

In 1961, the new owners of Frontier Motel, 5510 New Sapulpa Road, wanted to operate as a rest and care home for the elderly. When that plan fell apart, it returned to overnight guests in 1962. It has operated as the Crystal Motel since 1977. Note the road sign showing the distance to the turnpike entrance. (Courtesy of Mike Ward.)

Rio Motor Hotel, 2222 West Skelly Drive, built by Oklahoma City developer William C. Collins, opened concurrently with Interstate 44 in 1958. An outstanding feature of this 80-room, two-level complex was the unique mid-century modern sculptures in the courtyard. The motel operates in 2025 as Royal Inn Express, with the cool architectural touches intact. (Courtesy of Steve Clem.)

Oil Capital Motel, on Interstate 44 west of the Pepsi plant, had a 24-hour pumping oil well from Bethlehem Steel and a large neon sign, which has been replicated for the Avery Plaza Southwest neon sign park. A former employee remembers getting business from the Bellaire Drive-In theater across the street and seeing bootlegger Cleo Epps peddling her wares in the parking lot. It is now a Budget Inn. (Courtesy of Joe Sonderman.)

After the 330-room Camelot Inn opened in 1965 at Interstate 44 and Peoria Avenue, overnight visitors could claim to have slept in a castle. Built in the style of a medieval English castle, the $5 million hotel hosted events and was shown in the movie *Tex*. Elvis Presley and presidents Richard Nixon and Gerald Ford also slept there. It was demolished in 2007. (Courtesy of Beryl Ford Collection/Rotary Club of Tulsa.)

Built by W.D. Armstrong for $300,000 in 1958–1959, the Valley Inn was advertised as "Tulsa's futuristic look at roadside living." Located at 1347 East Skelly Drive, just east of the Bellaire Shopping Center and adjacent to the US 66 Bypass, it had 90 rooms, an outdoor pool, and a 24-hour restaurant. The motel operates in the modern era as LTA Suites. (Courtesy of Steve Clem.)

Tulsan Robert S. Mitchell built the Flamingo and Desert Hills motor courts on East Eleventh Street, then the Sands, Town and Country, and Western Capri motels on Interstate 44 before hitting his stride with the distinctive and popular Trade Winds chain of motor hotels. All three Tulsa Trade Winds were within a few miles of each other along Interstate 44, which resulted in frequent reservation calamities. With a focus on service, the Trade Winds featured large rooms and suites, convention facilities, and clubs on site, including the Tiki Nook at Trade Winds West, Fifty-First Street and Peoria Avenue, and Elephant Run at Trade Winds Central, Interstate 44 at Harvard Avenue, which still operates as Trade Winds Inn. At left, the sign for Trade Winds East is pictured. Shown below are the mid-century modern furnishings inside the 300-room Trade Winds West. (Both, courtesy of Beryl Ford Collection/Rotary Club of Tulsa.)

Over its 28 years in business, from 1958 to 1986, countless couples spent their wedding night in the honeymoon suite at the Ramada Roadside Inn, Interstate 44 at South Yale Avenue. When the luxury motel shuttered in 1986, the French Provincial furnishings, fixtures, and even the bricks were sold at salvage. One gentleman purchased the door to the room where he and his wife had honeymooned. (Courtesy of Steve Clem.)

In November 1962, the *Tulsa Tribune* announced that the Rodeway Inn, the first of 30 motels in a five-state area to be built by Tulsa attorney E.H. Gubser, would soon commence construction on the south side of Skelly Drive between Harvard and Yale Avenues. "The exterior will be brick architecture, patterned after the colonial restoration at Williamsburg, Va., with furnishings in early American style." (Courtesy of Mike Ward.)

As Tulsa's population migrated south to the interstate and beyond, entertainment venues followed. In the mid-1960s, Oklahoma City–based Barton Theatres brought back elegance to the movie experience with the Continental, Interstate 44 at Memorial Drive. It had a 900-seat auditorium with plush oversized seats and a giant, curved Cinerama screen. The theater specialized in showing films from large 70-mm prints with an intermission. It closed in 1981. (Courtesy of Museum of Tulsa History.)

Matchbooks, often with bold designs like this one, were freebies. Howard Johnson's Motor Lodge, Interstate 44 near South Garnett Road, opened in 1974. Later operating as Econo Lodge and finally, Oaktree Inn, the former convention hotel became a hub for criminal activity. A 2019 proposal to rehab the five-building complex into offices, retail, and a marijuana-growing facility stalled, and the property was razed. (Courtesy of Steve Clem.)

Six

Michael Wallis

Mother Road Renaissance and the Sheriff of Radiator Springs

Award-winning journalist Michael Wallis was working out of the Caribbean bureau for *Time* magazine when he first visited Tulsa during a heat wave in June 1980. Despite triple-digit temperatures, Wallis liked what he saw—the Arkansas River, the great inventory of Art Deco architecture, and the Mother Road.

Wallis and his wife, Suzanne Fitzgerald Wallis, moved to Tulsa in 1982. By the late 1980s, the writer began hearing people talk about Route 66 in the past tense. US Highway 66 had been replaced by the Interstate Highway System and decertified in 1985. Officially, the route no longer existed.

However, Wallis knew that 85 percent of the route was still out there and drivable. "I knew Ted Drewes was still serving up that wonderful ambrosia at his custard stand in St Louis. I knew Angel Delgadillo was still cutting hair and shaving faces in Seligman. I knew Lilian Redman was switching on those neon blue swallows in Tucumcari," Wallis recalled. "And I knew that outside of Tulsa, there was a big, smiling whale!"

When Wallis's book *Route 66: The Mother Road* was published in 1990, it was a phenomenon. Additional print runs were needed during the initial promotional tour. Eventually selling one million copies, it earned Wallis his first of three Pulitzer Prize nominations. It also did something not measurable by sales statistics or industry accolades. It began the rebirth. The book sparked a worldwide renaissance of Route 66.

Wallis's book caught the attention of filmmaker John Lasseter, then chief creative officer for Pixar, the animation studio behind *Toy Story*. Lasseter was working on a movie involving the Mother Road. Flying out to Pixar's Emeryville, California, campus to meet Lasseter and the *Cars* development team, Wallis informed them that to write about Route 66, they had to go out and experience the road.

Wallis led Pixar story and art teams down Route 66 to draw inspiration from the characters and locales for what would become the movie *Cars*, released in 2006. It spawned two sequels and the attraction Cars Land at Disney California Adventure Park, which debuted in 2012.

At the conclusion of their trip down Route 66, Lasseter had a surprise for Wallis, who had guided the group and regaled them with stories along the way.

Route 66 flows through Michael Wallis's veins like a 1955 Plymouth threading the tight turns of old Missouri 66. Wallis grew up in St. Louis, just off the route. As a child, he took Highway 66 to visit his aunt and uncle in Chicago. It was also where he went on the big yellow school bus up to see Lincoln's tomb in Illinois. And his first car—the Plymouth—was purchased in Pacific, Missouri, on Route 66. At left, Wallis, age six, is already showing a love for the West. Below, Wallis (standing, third from right) poses with his fellow Marines at Camp Pendleton, California, in 1966. When Wallis hitchhiked home, one can guess which road he traveled. (Both, courtesy of Michael and Suzanne Wallis.)

Michael Wallis began his journalism career in the late 1960s as a freelancer and daily newspaper reporter. His byline appeared in hundreds of publications, including *People*, the *Smithsonian*, and the *New York Times*. At right, Michael and Suzanne relax in El Paso, Texas, in 1969. (Courtesy of James W. Fitzgerald, Jr.)

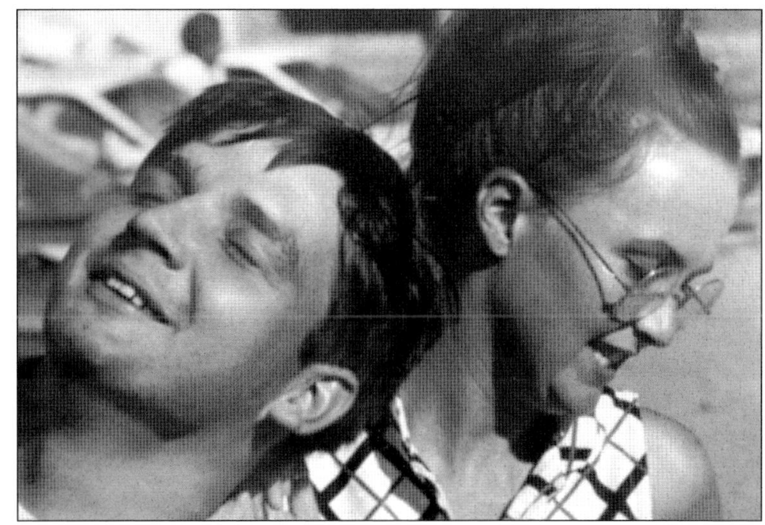

Says Wallis, second from left in the photograph, "Filled with the spirit that drove Ken Kesey and his Merry Pranksters, we formed the Spinners with other artists and writers. On January 2, 1970, we struck out for Taos to meet the revered painter Dorothy Brett and asked her how we could launch a major cultural movement." (Courtesy of Michael and Suzanne Wallis.)

After Wallis completed his first book, *Oil Man: The Story of Frank Phillips and the Birth of Phillips Petroleum*, the writer was searching for his next subject. Around that time, in the late 1980s, he began to hear people speak about Route 66 in the past tense. So, he composed a love letter. "I called it a love letter to the highway but not just the physical highway, the varicose asphalt, but the people of the highway," Wallis recalled. Released in 1990, *Route 66: The Mother Road* became a *Los Angeles Times* and *New York Times* bestseller. On the national tour to promote the book, there were interviews on CNN and *Good Morning America*, and three additional print runs were needed to meet the demand. At left, Wallis is pictured with the CEO of Tulsa's Community Bank, Morris Permenter. (Left, courtesy of Oklahoma Historical Society; below, courtesy of Shellee Graham.)

Wallis led the Pixar creative team down Route 66 to scout characters and locales that would help inspire the movie *Cars*. "We were in three big Detroit sleds, big Cadillacs," Wallis remembered. Wallis liked to stop every 300 yards for activities like removing box turtles from the roadway and picking wild grapes. Entering Galena, Kansas, the entourage stopped at Main Street. "The group walked around to absorb people, write notes, and photograph things," Wallis explained. "I walked up behind this old derelict building up in the weeds and there sat this old, rusted tow truck." Wallis summoned Lasseter and the team. "They saw it and their mouths fell open and I knew that that vehicle would be in the film. Of course, that was Tow Mater," Wallis beamed. (Both, courtesy of Pixar Animation Studios, the Walt Disney Company.)

After their cross-country journey, Lasseter informed Wallis that the Pixar team loved his voice and wanted it in the film. They cast him in the role of Sheriff of Radiator Springs, which Wallis has voiced in three *Cars* films to date. Above, Wallis gives a presentation at the Heart of Route 66 Museum in Sapulpa, Oklahoma. The filmmaker also asked Michael and Suzanne to write the accompanying book for the film, *The Art of Cars*, by Chronicle Books, a beautiful volume that features storyboards, snapshots, and hundreds of character sketches from the making of the film. (Above, courtesy of Ken Busby; below, courtesy of Pixar Animation Studios, the Walt Disney Company.)

Disney presents a PIXAR film

THE ART OF Cars

©2006 Disney

By Michael Wallis with Suzanne Fitzgerald Wallis

Foreword by Pixar's John Lasseter

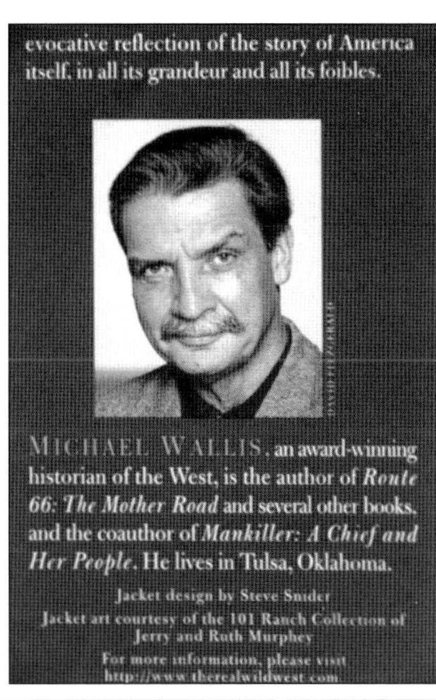

evocative reflection of the story of America itself, in all its grandeur and all its foibles.

MICHAEL WALLIS, an award-winning historian of the West, is the author of *Route 66: The Mother Road* and several other books, and the coauthor of *Mankiller: A Chief and Her People*. He lives in Tulsa, Oklahoma.

Jacket design by Steve Snider
Jacket art courtesy of the 101 Ranch Collection of Jerry and Ruth Murphey
For more information, please visit http://www.therealwildwest.com

Michael Wallis is one of the nation's premier journalists on the American West. He excels in tackling historical figures steeped in mythology, peeling back the layers of legend through meticulous research to reveal the real person. Wallis's three Pulitzer Prize nominations came for *Route 66: The Mother Road*; *Pretty Boy: The Life and Times of Charles Arthur Floyd*; and *Mankiller: A Chief and Her People*. Wallis's 20th book, *Belle Starr: The Truth Behind the Wild West Legend*, was released in 2025. At right is the back jacket to Wallis's *The Real Wild West: The 101 Ranch and the Creation of the American West*. Below, Wallis speaks at the Oklahoma Route 66 Museum in Clinton, Oklahoma, in 2016. (Right, courtesy of David Fitzgerald; below, courtesy of Shellee Graham.)

Through the Route 66 Alliance, Michael Wallis and executive director Ken Busby work for the betterment of the entire 2,448 miles of the Mother Road. Wallis is also a constant presence at Tulsa Route 66 triumphs, whether it is a ceremony rededicating a lost historical marker for the Sue A. Bland No. 1 oil strike in Red Fork, launch parties for Buck Atom and Stella Atom, or events honoring Cyrus Avery, the "Father of Route 66." Above, Wallis speaks at the 2004 dedication of the Cyrus Avery Route 66 Memorial Bridge with, from left to right, Marion Clark, author of the *Route 66 Cookbook*; Joy Avery, granddaughter of Cyrus Avery; Cyrus Stevens Avery II, grandson; Cyrus Stevens Avery III; Ella Jane Avery; and Allyson Anne Avery. Below, Busby interviews Wallis at the AAA Road Fest in 2022. (Above, courtesy of Shellee Graham; below, courtesy of Route 66 Alliance.)

In the 1990s, Michael Wallis gained a reputation for marrying people on Route 66. However, there was a catch. The weddings were only good for the weekend. After one couple requested a forever wedding, Wallis gained the credentials and has married five couples. On April 21, 2017, Wallis attended Route 66 Neon Fest in Arcadia, Oklahoma, in the backyard neon garden, above, of Route 66 authors and preservationists Jim Ross and Shellee Graham. At dusk on that cool, misty evening, Wallis said it would be a fine night for a wedding and asked for volunteers. As the crowd milled around, the groom, Jim Ross, stepped forward, and the bride-to-be, Shellee Graham, emerged from the house with her bridesmaids for their pop-up wedding, officiated by Wallis. (Above, courtesy of Steve Clem; right, courtesy of Shellee Graham/Phyllis Grey.)

Juniper, a blonde cat, and Martini, a black feline, shown at left, serve as Wallis's literary muses. In 2022, Wallis received a belated Christmas present. On December 28 that year, Pres. Joe Biden appointed him to the Route 66 Centennial Commission, the group established by Congress to recommend activities to celebrate the centennial anniversary of the Mother Road in 2026. In Tulsa, it has been a long road—pun intended—from Wallis's 1990 book that began the movement to the full-blown renaissance enjoyed today in the Capital of Route 66. Below is a portrait of Suzanne and Michael Wallis. (Both, courtesy of Michael and Suzanne Wallis.)

Seven

Capital of Route 66

Investment, Neon, and a Cowboy Named Buck

In 2024, after a century of becoming and two years of filling out the paperwork, Tulsa officially assumed the title of Capital of Route 66.

It is a title born of the spirit of Cyrus Avery, the "Father of Route 66"—his passion to plan, create, and promote the highway that first captured the imagination of a nation and then the world.

The title honors an earlier capital, one created by oil, that built a thriving city on an Art Deco playground.

It is the embodiment of the wanderlust spirit that must discover what is just down the road or around the next corner.

Capital of Route 66 evokes the memory of the moms and pops of the past who dispensed Tulsa hospitality with every room key, of mechanics who gave passing-through motorists a fighting chance to make Amarillo by dark, and waitresses who called one "darlin' " while topping off their cup.

Capital of Route 66 honors a Tulsan who wrote about the Mother Road so eloquently that the whole world took notice. It celebrates a city invested in the route's future with brilliant neon that lights up the night and illuminates its history.

It acknowledges architects who saw gold in a huge, old, roached-out neon sign, and celebrates preservationists who save what they can and re-create or reimagine the rest.

Capital of Route 66 celebrates the entrepreneurial spirit—alive in the visionaries whose imaginations and hard work make traveling Historic Route 66 in Tulsa a special experience. And it provides the foundation for future enterprises that will define Tulsa's Route 66.

It is a title that comes to life with each camera click that preserves a precious memory made in the Capital of Route 66.

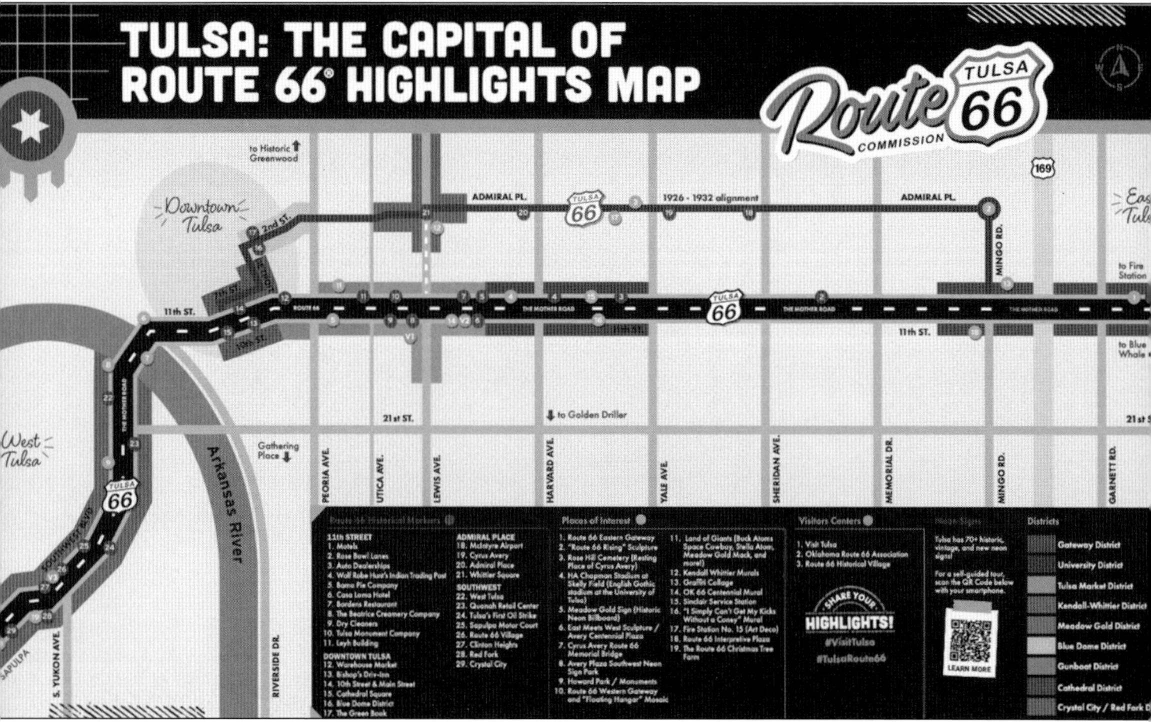

In Tulsa, as in other Route 66 cities, the historic alignments of the Mother Road experienced a prolonged period of decline after Route 66 moved to the interstate and populations shifted to south Tulsa and the suburbs. At the dawn of the new millennium, much of Eleventh Street and Admiral Place were defined by urban blight. In 2003, voters passed Vision 2025, a Tulsa County sales tax that devoted $15 million to Tulsa Route 66 projects. One initiative, the city's Neon Sign Grant Program, provided businesses along the historic alignments with up to 50 percent matching funds for neon sign repair or new signs. Several dozen businesses have benefited, illuminating the historic routes. In 2024, Tulsa officially became the Capital of Route 66. Businesses and entrepreneurs understand the value of being on Route 66, and travelers, who previously bypassed Tulsa on Interstate 44, exit the interstate to experience the Mother Road capital. This map shows both historic alignments, points of interest, and the location of Route 66 historical markers and neon signs. (Courtesy of Tulsa Route 66 Commission.)

Vision 2025 funds financed gateways that bookend Tulsa's Historic Route 66. The eastern gateway is on East Eleventh Street east of South Garnett Road. Its LED Route 66 shield lights up at night. (Courtesy of Steve Clem.)

A Tulsa fire station at the city's eastern edge has been rebranded Fire Station 66, and its motto identifies the station's firefighters as "Keepers of the Mother Road." A large Route 66 sign and vintage fire truck that once served downtown Tulsa present a photo opportunity near the capital city's eastern entrance. (Courtesy of Steve Clem.)

It is hallowed ground on Tulsa's Mother Road—the spot where the "Father of Route 66," Cyrus Avery, had his 1920s gas station and restaurant. Once at the intersection of Admiral Place and Mingo Road, that complex was razed in 1943. Now, the eye-catching 70-foot-by-30-foot sculpture by artist Eric F. Garcia, *Route 66 Rising*, dedicated in 2019, welcomes worldwide travelers around that special space. (Courtesy of Steve Clem.)

The Capital of Route 66 features a dynamic blend of architecture, including Art Deco (Zigzag, Works Progress Administration [WPA], and Streamline) and Gothic as well as space-age signs from the 1960s. One of the city's most photographed neon signs is this c. 1960 sign for Oasis Motel, 9303 East Eleventh Street. An example of the Googie style, it features sharp, bold, geometric angles and shapes. (Courtesy of Rhys Martin.)

A giant driller was a tradition at Tulsa International Petroleum Expositions, held in Tulsa between 1923 and 1979. The 1966 event brought a permanent Golden Driller, symbolizing the city's oil industry prowess. Constructed of steel covered with concrete and plaster, at 76 feet, the statue is three times taller than a muffler man giant. (Courtesy of John Margolies Roadside America archive [1972–2008], Library of Congress.)

Since opening on the Mother Road in 1987 on the southwest corner of Eleventh Street and Yale Avenue, Tally's Good Food Café has become a gathering spot for travelers. Citizens of other countries who have saved for years to cruise Route 66 mingle with locals who have scraped together a few bucks for breakfast. Cinnamon rolls are a Tally's delicacy. (Courtesy of Brady A. Wilson.)

The many gasoline stations from Tulsa's oil era provide numerous candidates for adaptive reuse. Two outstanding examples are the Sinclair Station at 3501 East Eleventh Street, above, and Cities Service Station No. 8 at 1648 Southwest Boulevard, below. Oilman Harry Sinclair developed the bank that eventually became the National Bank of Tulsa and established the Sinclair Oil Company. The 1929 Sinclair station shown above, built in the Spanish Eclectic style, now houses Rossi Brothers Doors and Windows. While the original Cities Service Station dates to 1926, an expansion in 1940 and a renovation in the 1950s gave the building a rectangular shape and a new Modern Movement style. Tulsa attorney Jim Frasier purchased and restored the neglected building in the early 2000s; it now houses an architectural firm. Each station is in the National Register of Historic Places. (Both, courtesy of Steve Clem.)

This structure in the National Register of Historic Places predates Eleventh Street as Route 66. The block-long Spanish Mission–style Casa Loma Hotel went up in 1927, with retail shops at ground level and a hotel above. After sitting empty for years after Route 66 moved to Interstate 44, the historic building was reborn as the boutique Campbell Hotel with themed rooms in 2011. (Courtesy of Steve Clem.)

When Mother Road Market opened in November 2018 on the southwest corner of East Eleventh Street and South Lewis Avenue, it became an instant destination. The Lobeck Taylor Family Foundation's 27,000-square-foot food hall's recipe is fun cuisine choices, new restaurant concepts, unique retail, a bar, and a spacious patio area with Route 66–themed miniature golf. (Courtesy of Steve Clem.)

In 1993, when Home Depot decided to build downtown, it chose a historic site: Eleventh Street and Elgin Avenue. It had been McNulty Park before the Public Market building came in 1930. At a cost of $1 million, the home improvement retailer saved the decaying structure's stunning Art Deco facade and decorative tower. At left, a portion of the front decorative work is shown. (Courtesy of Steve Clem.)

After opening in downtown Tulsa in 1950, El Rancho Grande moved to its current location on Route 66, just west of Utica Avenue, in 1953. Operating for over 70 years, it is the longest-running eatery on Tulsa's 28 miles of historic Mother Road. Captivating neon and crowd-pleasing cuisine have served this business well. (Courtesy of Steve Clem.)

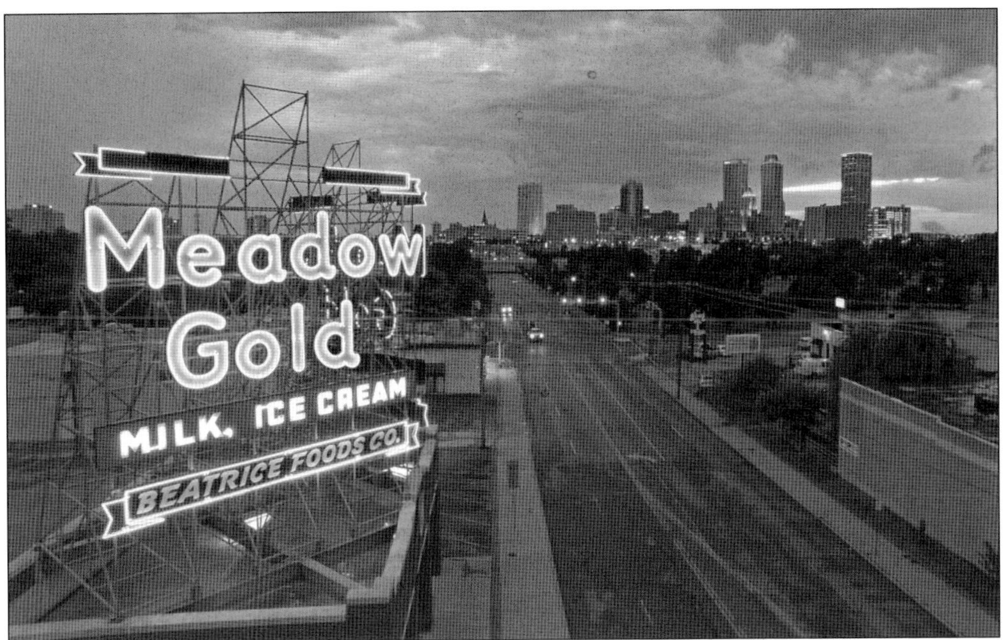

This Meadow Gold dairy sign dates to 1934 on Tulsa's Route 66. In 2004, the Tulsa Foundation for Architecture was set to restore the landmark when a new owner announced plans to demolish it. Several organizations united to save the spectacular neon, which now anchors the Meadow Gold District on Eleventh Street, just east of Peoria. It is shown before the reproduction clocks were added. (Courtesy of Michael Hardeman.)

Decopolis, 1401 East Eleventh Street, is Tulsan William Franklin's magical haven of hidden rooms and treasures that includes a volcano, cave, dinosaurs, and rocks and fossils. Decopolis also carries sci-fi and fantasy gifts, along with books and toys. In 2025, Franklin announced plans for a second location a few miles east to house the newest, magically themed Decopolis attractions and Tulsa's Art Deco Museum. (Courtesy of Steve Clem.)

Entrepreneur Mary Beth Babcock became enamored with the Mother Road at her retail shop, Dwelling Spaces, on the route's original alignment from 2006 to 2016. When a 1950s PEMCO gas station became available, Babcock jumped at the chance to have a souvenir shop in a service station on Route 66. Needing a mascot, she conceived Buck Atom Space Cowboy, and Mark Cline of Enchanted Castle Studios realized her vision in a 21-foot-tall muffler man. Since landing in May 2019, Buck and his friends have pulled tourists off the interstate to the heart of Historic 66 on East Eleventh Street. (Both, courtesy of Melissa Winterscheid.)

In June 2024, Mary Beth Babcock added a space cowgirl to her gift shop, Stella Atom. Mark Cline made the 17.5-foot-tall statue from an original Uniroyal Gal mold. Where the Uniroyal giant's raised hand would have held a tire, Stella grips a ray gun and wears a jet pack, creations of Josh Waddell of 3 Bulls UPcycling, LLC. Her cuff was contributed by Beverly Wissen of Genuine Oklahoma Souvenirs. Below, Babcock poses with a miniature of Meadow Gold Mack, another giant project. (Both, courtesy of Steve Clem.)

Mary Beth Babcock teamed with a Tulsa developer on an original muffler man from the 1960s that they named Meadow Gold Mack the Friendly Lumberjack. The 20-foot-tall axe-wielding giant took his place next to the historic Meadow Gold sign, across the street from Buck and Stella Atom, in August 2024. The following year, two more giants were installed in the Meadow Gold District: Cowboy Bob at the new Buck's Vintage and Rosie the Riveter at Ike's Chili. (Courtesy of Steve Clem.)

One of the coolest new signs to come from the Tulsa Neon Sign Grant Program is the "spinning record" signage of Josey Records on East Eleventh Street and South Rockford Avenue. This, and other brilliant new neons, has helped elevate the Capital of Route 66 to a desired destination both day and night. (Courtesy of Steve Clem.)

On the Cyrus Avery Centennial Plaza at the northern terminus of Riverside Drive stands the 20,000-pound bronze sculpture *East Meets West*. It depicts the Avery family in a 1926 Ford in a surprise meeting with a horse-drawn wagon loaded with oil field supplies. Dedicated in 2012 with Avery descendants in attendance, the 135-percent-scaled outdoor installation by sculptor Robert Summers features 1,000 pieces of bronze, including a flattened grasshopper on the radiator grille. The meeting of car and wagon symbolizes the all-too-real intersection of downtown oil and business interests with the blue-collar workers of Tulsa's Westside as well as the eastern US landscapes of trees and hills meeting the western prairies and deserts. Below, at the west end of the Cyrus Avery Route 66 Memorial Bridge, three lost neons are recreated: Oil Capital Motel, Tulsa Auto Court, and Will Rogers Motor Court. (Both, courtesy of Steve Clem.)

Oklahoma's native son Will Rogers was America's most widely read columnist at the time of his 1935 death. His homespun humor and commentary appeared in over 500 newspapers. After his untimely passing, Tulsans began the movement to rename Route 66 the Will Rogers Highway, which occurred the following year. In 1952, to promote *The Story of Will Rogers* movie, a caravan traveled the route rechristening the Mother Road as the Will Rogers Highway. In 2001, this polished granite marker, featuring a Michael Wallis quote, was placed near Howard Park to honor the humorist and actor born 30 miles northeast of Tulsa. (Courtesy of Steve Clem.)

Three limestone monoliths, sculpted by artist Patrick Sullivan in 2017, are hidden gems on Tulsa's Route 66. In historic Howard Park on Southwest Boulevard, these hand-carved columns of Indiana limestone, standing nearly 10 feet tall, tell Tulsa's history of transportation, industry, Indigenous peoples, aviation, and culture. In 2025, Tulsa Route 66 Main Street announced plans for a 66-foot dinosaur sculpture, designed and built by Mark Cline, to be installed in Howard Park. (Courtesy of Becky Hatchett.)

The first Route 66 Neon Sign Grant Program recipient was Billy Ray's Catfish and Barbeque, located at 3524 Southwest Boulevard. Billy Ray Cooper opened the restaurant in 1984 and would often greet customers in his overalls as they walked in the door. His wife, Sherry, shown at the neon relighting ceremony, took over after Cooper's passing in 2017. (Courtesy of Steve Clem.)

In 1983, Ollie Hibdon opened a restaurant at 4070 Southwest Boulevard. In 1987, John Gray put the restaurant on the Route 66 must-see map when he began decorating the interior with model trains and railroad memorabilia, perfect for its location just blocks from the original 1883 Red Fork railroad depot. Joe Gilling, owner since 2004, continues serving comfort food with a dash of entertainment. (Courtesy of Becky Hatchett.)

The history of transportation in Tulsa is again a theme at the Route 66 Historical Village, an outdoor museum that includes a steam engine, passenger car, caboose, and oil tank car that represent Tulsa's railroad history. The new Red Fork Depot serves as an event center. Getting the train cars onto the grounds in 2011 was a sight to behold. It involved preparing the track at the village that would receive the train cars, closing Southwest Boulevard to traffic while crews laid

track across the road, then moving the engine and cars from the Tulsa Sapulpa Union tracks across the highway. The village's location on Route 66 is celebrated with a 1920s-style filling station, and Tulsa's oil history is represented by the tallest oil derrick in North America, constructed in 2007 to celebrate Oklahoma's centennial. (Courtesy of Steve Clem.)

Saved by a grassroots effort and restored by volunteers, the 405-ton Frisco 4500 steam engine now greets visitors at the Route 66 Historical Village. This image shows it decorated for Christmas. From 1942 to 1947, it pulled the passenger train *Meteor* from St. Louis to Oklahoma City daily, conveying newlyweds on honeymoons, businessmen to important meetings, and soldiers to their posts and home from World War II. (Courtesy of Brady A. Wilson.)

This replica of a 1920s–1930s Phillips 66 filling station serves as the Welcome Center for the Route 66 Historical Village. The Tudor cottage design was popularized by the Phillips Petroleum Company to incorporate its service stations into existing neighborhoods. The Phillips 66 brand of gasoline was named in 1927 when a car testing the fuel reached a speed of 66 miles per hour on Route 66. (Courtesy of Becky Hatchett.)

Tulsa's western gateway is at Crystal City Shopping Center, the former site of Crystal City Amusement Park, once a playground for locals and Route 66 travelers alike. A historical marker stands where kids splashed in the giant pool and rammed each other with Dodgem bumper cars. A 10-foot sculpture by Reno artist Eileen Gay features two rotary gears from the oil field with a mosaic of a train engine and an oil well pumpjack. There is so much history here in the city where Cyrus Avery realized his dream of a Chicago to Los Angeles thoroughfare that traversed his hometown of Tulsa, where east meets west, in the Capital of Route 66! (Both, courtesy of Steve Clem.)